# Bach Flower Remedies
# For
# Animals

# Bach Flower Remedies For Animals

by

## Helen Graham & Gregory Vlamis

FINDHORN
*Press*

First published in 1999


ISBN 1-899171-72-X

British Library Cataloguing-in-Publication Data.
A catalogue record for this book is available from the British Library.


Layout by Pam Bochel
Cover design by Phoenix Graphics

Printed and bound by WSOY, Finland




Published by

**Findhorn Press**

| The Park, Findhorn, | P.O. Box 13939 |
| Forres IV36 3TY | Tallahassee |
| Scotland | Florida 32317-3939, USA |
| Tel 01309 690582 | Tel 850 893 2920 |
| Fax 01309 690036 | Fax 850 893 3442 |

e-mail: info@findhornpress.com
http://www.findhornpress.com

## ACKNOWLEDGMENTS

Many individuals have graciously given their time to share their experiences and understanding of the mental and emotional aspects of animals and of the human–animal bond. The authors would like to acknowledge those who have shared their insights, made interesting observations, and found unique ways to use flower remedies/essences in the treatment of animals.

This work would not exist had it not been for the system of treatment widely known as the Bach Flower Remedies developed by Dr. Edward Bach.

**WE ARE DEEPLY INDEBTED TO THE FOLLOWING US AND UK VETERINARY EXPERTS:**
Richard Blackman, B.V.Sc., MRCVS; Stephen Blake, DVM; Bruce Borland, B.Vet.Med., MRCVS; Christiana Chambreau, DVM; P.A. Culpin, MRCVS; Christopher Day, MA.Vet.MB, MRCVS, Vet.MFHOM; Gloria Dodd, DVM; Eric Foster, DVM; Anthony Frith, B.V.Sc.; Deva Khalsa, B.V.Sc.; Michael W. Lemmon, DVM; Jeffrey Levy, DVM; John B. Limehouse, DVM; George McLeod, DVSM, MRCVS (deceased); Dr. MacMichael, DVM; Myrna Milani, DVM; Yvonne Nelson, DVM; J.L. Newns, B.Vet.Med., MRCVS; Richard Pitcairn, DVM, Ph.D.; Norman C. Ralston, DVM; James Ratcliffe, BVMS, MRCVS; Anne Rice, DVM; John G.C. Saxton, B.Vet.Med, MRCVS; C. Schwartz, DVM; M.J. Statham, B.V.Sc., MRCVS; Joanne Stefanatos, DVM; Judith Swanson, DVM; Michelle Tilghman, DVM; Eileen Wheeler, MRCVS; W. Hugh Wheir, DVM; Will Winter, DVM; Ron Wolf, DVM; Neil C. Wolff, DVM.

**ALSO TO THE FOLLOWING FOR THEIR INSIGHTS:**
Robert M. Andrysco, Ph.D.; Maggie and Mary Asproyerakas; Fabio Biagi; Alenka Bradley; John Bryant; Kaye Cornish; Mrs Dowers; Ron Eager; John Fisher; Ruth Fisher; Barbara Block Frank; Sue Fuller; Jean Gibb; Lydia Hiby; Robyn Hood; Priscilla Hoback; Nick Jannes; Elizabeth Jonca; J. Jureit; Judy Kaufner; Sheri Kennedy; Rebekah Leonhart: Pat Lester; Beatrice Lydecker; Marika and Marianna McCausland; Robyn Michaels; Sheila Morgan; Roger Mugford, BSC, Ph.D.; Peter and Claire Bessant Neville; Karen Okura; Nora O'Sullivan; John Ottaviano, OMD; Penny Peltz; Zorena B. Penalba; John Ramsell; Anne S. Rice; Brenda Rice; George Santos; Penelope Smith; Bob Stevens; Violet Todd; Victor Toso; Wendy Volhard; Ann Walker; Karen Webster; A. Whidden-Winter; Jean White; Dr. Marsha Woolf.

**A SPECIAL THANK YOU TO:**
Sue Smith, veterinary nurse; Penny Case, horse rehabilitation specialist; Barbara Meyers, holistic animal consultant; Harjinder Singh, DVM; Debbie Mills; Ralph and Leslie Kaslof; the late Nickie Murray, former curator of the Bach Centre; Livija Carlson and Lisa Berg of the University of Minnesota Veterinary Library; Lea Spencer; Paul Zuziak; and the Dr. Edward Bach Memorial Trust.

## NOTE TO THE READER

## TRADEMARKS AND DISCLAIMER

# CONTENTS

Introduction                                                                7

Part I:   Flower Essences in the Treatment of Animals
          Chapter One: What Are Flower Essences?                            11
          Chapter Two: How Can Flower Essences Help Animals?               21

Part II:  The Flower Essence Directory
                    Agrimony                                                33
                    Aspen                                                   35
                    Beech                                                   38
                    Centaury                                               40
                    Cerato                                                 41
                    Cherry Plum                                            42
                    Chestnut Bud                                           44
                    Chicory                                                45
                    Clematis                                               46
                    Crab Apple                                             47
                    Elm                                                    50
                    Gentian                                                52
                    Gorse                                                  53
                    Heather                                                54
                    Holly                                                  55
                    Honeysuckle                                            56
                    Hornbeam                                               57
                    Impatiens                                              58
                    Larch                                                  60

Mimulus                                    61

Mustard                                    62

Oak                                        64

Olive                                      65

Pine                                       67

Red Chestnut                               67

Rock Rose                                  68

Rock Water                                 69

Scleranthus                                72

Star of Bethlehem                          73

Sweet Chestnut                             74

Vervain                                    76

Vine                                       77

Walnut                                     80

Water Violet                               82

White Chestnut                             83

Wild Oat                                   84

Wild Rose                                  85

Willow                                     86

Emergency Remedies                         87

Flower Essence Summary Chart               94

Part III: Directions for Use

How to Choose the Correct Remedy or Remedy Combination   99

Administration and Dosage                  105

Appendix: Resource Guide                   109

References                                 111

Reading list                               115

Index                                      117

# Introduction

Christine was very concerned about Amber, her 13-year-old Labrador bitch, a much-loved family pet, who until recently had seemed well in herself and still able to enjoy life, despite a degree of deafness and loss of sight. Having always been very clean indoors, she now seemed reluctant to leave the house to relieve herself but became so excited when family members or visitors entered the house that she lost control of her bladder and became distressed afterwards. Christine was anxious in case these might be indications that Amber's health was beginning to fail, but more worried that if she consulted her vet, he would recommend that Amber be put to sleep simply because of her age and disabilities.

Christine found herself facing the same dilemma as many caring animal owners. How could she strike the proper balance between giving her pet every opportunity to enjoy its life to the full and prevent its suffering unnecessarily? Christine decided to try flower remedies and asked Helen's advice. Helen recommended a combination of flower remedies for Amber – Aspen for her reluctance to go out of the house, Larch to promote her confidence and Crab Apple to restore her dignity. Christine was also advised to take Elm herself to help her deal with the situation and Cerato to help her trust her own judgment regarding Amber's condition.

Forty-eight hours later, an exuberant Christine reported a remarkable change in Amber's well-being, and in her own feelings about the situation. Amber was now asking to go out regularly and she had been completely clean indoors. She also seemed to have regained much of her zest for life. Christine felt much more optimistic about Amber's condition and confident that she had not yet reached the situation where euthanasia needed to be considered. Many months later, Amber was still enjoying life to the full and giving pleasure to her owners.

How different this story might have been if Amber had not been given flower remedies. At worst she might have been put to sleep prematurely, if only to prevent further distress and inconvenience to her owner. She might have been given various drugs in an attempt to control her incontinence — drugs with potentially undesirable side effects. In either event, the financial and emotional cost to Christine would have been considerable.

Many animals are not as fortunate as Amber. Those whose problems, whether physical or behavioral, appear intractable may be destroyed. Every year millions of animals, often physically fit and healthy ones, are destroyed to give their human companions peace and rest from incontinence, unruliness, excessive noisiness, aggression, possessiveness, destructiveness, or other problems. A behavior problem is thus often a "terminal disease". Indeed, euthanasia for behavior problems is the main cause of death in young animals, and many people regard it as a treatment. Those whose owners cannot bring themselves to destroy the animal, for emotional or financial reasons, may simply discard it. The cost of veterinary attention also means that many animals are discarded or neglected by their owners. The price in animal and human suffering and in welfare services is incalculable. It is also avoidable. Correcting the behavior problem often saves an animal's life as effectively as surgery or other medical procedures and greatly reduces the suffering of all concerned. This does not require expensive behavior therapy or extensive behavior modification on the part of the owner – it can be brought about in many cases quite simply and inexpensively through the use of flower remedies. This book aims to provide you with essential information about the use of flower remedies in the treatment of animals.

# PART I

# Flower Essences
# in the
# Treatment of Animals

# Chapter One

# What Are Flower Essences?

*Little flower – but if I could understand what you are,*

*Root and all, and all in all*

*I should know what God and Man is.*

*Tennyson (Flower in the Crannied Wall, 1869)*

In all parts of the world since the earliest times flowering trees, shrubs, and herbs have been used for healing purposes. All parts of plants have been used. Ginseng, a substance derived from the aromatic roots of *Panax schinseng* or *Panax quinquefolius*, has long been used medicinally in China and is now widely used in the West. Quinine, derived from cinchona bark, is used as a tonic, to relieve fever and pain, and in malaria therapy. Aspirin, also widely used to relieve pain, fever, and colds, and to reduce inflammation, derives from the stems of *Spiraea ulmaria*. The narcotic drug cocaine, widely used medicinally as a topical anesthetic, is derived from coca leaves. Two of the most powerful painkilling agents, morphine and codeine, are alkaloids extracted from the unripe seed capsules of the opium poppy, *Papaver somniferum*. The heart stimulant digitalis is prepared from the dried leaves or seeds of the foxglove. Linseed from the flax plant and mustard seed have long been used as poultices, and oils derived from various parts of plants have a wide variety of medicinal uses. However, throughout history, flowers, the crowning glory of plants, have been considered to embody the fundamental nature, or essential character, of the plant and to have particular healing powers.

The terms *health* and *healing* originate in words meaning whole and are closely related to the word *holy*. Etymologically, therefore, to be healthy is to be whole or holy and this reflects the traditional belief that in order to be healthy it is necessary to be attuned to, and in harmony with, both physical and spiritual realities. The white lotus, *Nymphaea lotus*, regarded as sacred by the ancient Egyptians, and a related plant, *Nelumbo nucifera*, the sacred lotus of India, China, and Tibet, represent this state of perfection, or holiness. To the Tibetans, the lotus flower is not merely a symbol of perfection, but a means of realizing it. They teach that there is a direct link between the essential nature of plants and our own essential nature, or soul, and that at an unconscious level we can make contact with our own essence through that of plants and so restore harmony within ourselves. Flowers therefore have a vital healing function.

## PRINCIPLES OF HEALING WITH FLOWER ESSENCES

The idea underpinning this teaching is that the essence of any phenomenon is its vibrational character, and that there is a fundamental resonance between the vibrational character of certain phenomena and aspects of human nature which can be used to restore harmony to the latter. The principle of resonance, whereby energies vibrating with a certain frequency and amplitude reverberate with similar energies in the environment, forms the basis of most traditional approaches to healing throughout the world. Yet its implications for healing are not generally accepted in contemporary Western thinking, despite the discoveries of physicists this century that describe all phenomena, including the physical body, as comprising nothing but energy in constant transformation. (Graham 1999) With this perspective it becomes easier to understand how the vibrational character of plants, or flower essences, can be used for healing purposes.

## SAMUEL HAHNEMANN AND HOMEOPATHY

Samuel Hahnemann (1755–1843), the German physician who founded homeopathy, understood this more than a century before it was established scientifically. He considered there to be certain basic vibrational patterns of disease, or miasms, that originate in the energy field surrounding an organism and influence all its energies, setting up patterns of disease in the organism's life and body. These miasms can be inherited genetically or acquired by resonance. The former in the genetic code and the latter in the form of bacterial or viral attack, toxic pollution, or environmental influence, can lie dormant for many years and flare up in times of stress or weakness. The organism then reacts to this disease or imbalance of its energies by attempting to restore balance. In so doing, it produces the symptoms and signs the patient feels and others observe. The homeopath, unlike the allopathic physician, doesn't consider these to be illnesses *per se* but the body's reaction to the original state of imbalance. They are an indication of the extent of the imbalance and of how profoundly the organism is affected by it. As such, they can be used to determine the treatments appropriate to restoring balance and hence health.

The homeopathic treatments developed by Hahnemann restore the balance of subtle energy fields of the body by matching various natural remedies of different vibrational characters with the disharmonies of the body, thereby restoring harmony or health to its energy pattern. These remedies, derived mostly from plants, animals, and minerals, utilize the principle of resonance, applying remedies which subject the organism to a periodic disturbance of the same frequency as that of the body. When this happens, the body displays an enhanced oscillation or vibration. Implicit in Hahnemann's system is the understanding that imbalances occurring in the body are symptomatic of energy imbalances occurring at more subtle levels, and that these imbalances first manifest at the psychological or emotional level – that is at a higher vibrational level than that of the physical or material body – and that energy imbalances successfully treated at this level do not manifest as symptoms at the physical level.

## HOMEOPATHY AND FLOWER ESSENCES

Systems of healing with flower essences utilize similar principles to homeopathy. Wright (1988, p.3) describes flower essences as "liquid pattern-infused solutions made from individual plant flowers, each containing a specific imprint that responds in a balancing, repairing and rebuilding manner to imbalances in humans on their physical, emotional, mental and spiritual or universal levels". This "imprint" is the vibrational character of the flower, as Leonardi (cited Morrison 1995, p.85) explains:

> It's commonly understood that everything in the universe has a vibration to it. What makes something red is its vibration. Scientifically, you'd say red is its vibration. Flowers have a certain frequency, too. If you process a flower into an essence and you take it into your body, it starts to vibrate at that frequency. It starts to create a synchronization of other cells and tissue in your body, causing them to vibrate at that level.

He likens the synchronization to the way a tuning fork behaves. If you strike one tuning fork you can cause one next to it to begin vibrating at the same frequency.

Kaminski and Katz (1992) compare the effects of flower essences to the experience of hearing a particularly moving piece of music. They indicate that sound vibrations may evoke emotions that indirectly affect physiological processes such as breathing, pulse rate, and other physical states. The modern interdisciplinary science of psychoneuroimmunology, or PNI (see Graham 1999), has confirmed the relationship between emotional and physical states. There is now abundant evidence that emotions produce changes in various hormones that trigger biochemical responses, which in turn bring about changes in nerve function, digestion, respiration, circulation, and the immune system (Pelletier & Herzing 1989). However, the role of flower essences in the processes being investigated in PNI has still to be established scientifically. As Morrison (1995) indicates, it needs to be shown first that infusions of flowers carry vibrations that trigger changes in the energy of the human body, and then that this particular energy change is related to emotions.

## THE INFLUENCE OF EDWARD BACH

Nevertheless, systems of healing with flower essences are numerous and widespread throughout the world (see Appendix I). Many of these are based on longstanding healing traditions. The first modern therapeutic system based on flower essences was developed by the distinguished British physician Edward Bach (1886–1936). From his two brief accounts (1931, 1936) of the development of flower essences as a system of treatment, it is clear Bach was greatly influenced by Hahnemann.

> *Disease will never be cured or eradicated by present materialistic methods, for the simple reason that disease in its origin is not material. What we know as disease is an ultimate result produced in the body, the end product of deep and long acting forces, and even if material treatment alone is apparently successful this is nothing more than a temporary relief unless the real cause has been removed. (1931, p.6)*

For Bach the "real" cause of disease is a distortion of the wavelength in the energy field of the body, which slows down, exerting an effect that results in negative states of mind such as worry, anxiety and impatience. These negative states so deplete the individual's vitality that the body loses its natural resistance and becomes vulnerable to infection and illness. Like Hahnemann, therefore, Bach believed that the patient should be treated rather than the disease, and the cause rather than its effects.

Hahnemann's influence on Bach is unsurprising because in 1919 Bach became a bacteriologist and pathologist at the London Homoeopathic Hospital, where he developed various oral bacterial vaccines, or nosodes, that are still widely used in homeopathic practice. His clinical experience confirmed his belief that disease is "the consolidation of mental attitude" and that mental attitude should be used as a guide to necessary treatment because the mind shows the onset and cause of disease more definitely and much sooner than the body. In 1930, aged 43, he gave up his Harley Street practice to search for an even more natural method of treatment than homeopathy, which did not require "anything to be destroyed or altered".

Bach's research led him to conclude that positive, healthy states of mind could be restored by the energies found in flowering plants, trees, bushes, and special waters. Initially, he discovered twelve healing herbs each with a natural affinity to certain mental traits. These, he believed, showed the same vibrational character as the quality concerned but without distortion and at the normal rhythm, and could be used to re-establish its harmonious vibration through the principle of resonance. Accordingly, by operating at subtle energy levels, these healing herbs can act as a catalyst for reintegration and healing. He went on to identify 38 healing remedies, which he believed could be used to remedy all the known negative states of mind that afflict humankind. He therefore considered his remedies to be a complete system of treatment requiring "no extension or alteration".

## PREPARING FLOWER ESSENCES

Bach collected and prepared most of the flowers used in his remedies from their natural habitat in many different areas of the English countryside. The exceptions were Cerato, a cultivated herb native to Tibet, and the remedies Olive and Vine, which grew in the warmer climate of the Mediterranean, which his friends sent him. He prepared these remedies for use in two ways: the sun method and the boiling method. He used the sun method for flowers blooming during the late spring and summer when the sun is at its height, and the boiling method for flowers from trees, bushes, and plants that bloom early in the year before there is much sunshine. For the sun method of preparation, flowers were picked around 9 A.M., placed in a clean, plain glass bowl full of clear spring water and left in full sunshine for three hours. The vitalized water was then added to bottles half-filled with brandy, which were tightly sealed and labelled. This "Mother Tincture", which would keep for many years, was then used to prepare stock bottles, each containing two drops of the original tincture in brandy.

In the boiling method, flowers were collected on a fine sunny morning around 9 A.M. and boiled in spring water before being treated in the same way (further details about the preparation of flower essences is provided by Barnard and Barnard 1996).

## Bach's Use of Flower Essences in Treatment

Bach tested each of his remedies on himself and his findings were subsequently verified by his colleague and friend, Dr. F. J. Wheeler, who used them in his own medical practice. Bach also treated many patients successfully with his remedies, and, as it was always his intention to make his system available to laymen as well as medical practitioners, he described it in several booklets (1931, 1933, 1934, 1936). He continued with this work until his death in 1936, and it has been continued in his name first by Mary Tabor, Victor Bullen, and Nora Weeks, then by John Ramsell and his sister Nickie Murray, and up to the present by John Ramsell, who although now retired, still assists his daughter, Judy Howard. The Bach Flower Remedies are now known and used worldwide in the treatment of people, but Bach insisted that his remedies could also be used effectively in treating plants and animals. An early account of their use in the treatment of animals was by Nora Weeks in 1939. As she later explained, "Animals suffer from moods in the same way as human beings, and so indicate their state of health... The Remedies help man and beast alike." (1942) They are now used extensively for this purpose.

## Recent Developments in the Preparation and Use of Flower Essences

Although Bach believed his system to be complete, in recent years other systems have been developed that are considerably more extensive. During the 1970s Richard Katz and Patricia Kaminski developed and produced the California Flower Essences and now direct the Flower Essence Society (FES). The FES markets 38 authentic essences called Healing Herbs English Flower Essences, which are made in the traditional manner according to Bach's instructions. Its repertory also includes 72 flower essences that are considered sufficiently well-described and understood to be reliably prescribed in the same way as the Bach Remedies and a further 24 essences with demonstrable healing properties that are less well-described and still at the research stage of development. As such, the *Flower Essence Repertory* (Kaminski & Katz, 1994) is the most comprehensive guide to North American and English flower essences currently available. The FES is also currently investigating a further 200 essences.

In the early 1980s, 112 flower essences were described in *Flower Essences and Vibrational Healing.* (Gurudas 1983) This acknowledged the important and inspirational contribution made by Edward Bach in developing his flower remedies but challenged the uniqueness and completeness claimed for his system. It argued that Bach had simply rediscovered in modern times ancient wisdom concerning the uses of flower essences in healing, and that had he lived longer he would have developed additional flower remedies. It provided detailed information on the preparation, storage, protection, amplification, and uses of each essence, together with an extensive discussion of how they actually work, their relationship with homeopathic and other remedies, and more information about the use of flower essences in the treatment of animals than any other source. Flower essences prepared according to the principles detailed in this book are distributed by Pegasus Products (USA). However, Stein (1993) observes that the remedies often duplicate, have uses too specific to be considered universal, or are too esoteric to be of real value in the treatment of animals. She cites as a case in point, Blue Flag essence, which is recommended for use "by pets whose creative people take the same essence for frustration".

The 1980s also saw the development of the Australian Bush Flower Essences by Ian White, who drew upon the traditional knowledge and use of flower essences by Australian Aborigines. White describes in great detail 50 flower remedies in his book *Australian Bush Flower Essences.* (1993) Like the remedies developed by Bach, these are based almost entirely on emotional characteristics and can be used in the treatment of animals.

The Alaskan Flower Essences were also developed during the 1980s by Steve Johnson. Mansfield (1995) suggests that they seem rather "ethereal", focusing mainly on mental and spiritual features. Certainly the keynotes provided to help users choose the correct remedy, such as "seeing through illusion", "perceptual expansion" and "greeting the earth", make their appropriateness in the treatment of animals somewhat questionable.

Machaelle Small Wright's Perelandra Flower Essences have been developed more recently. These are suitable for human and animal use. Stein (1993), who reports having used them extensively with animals, recommends them highly. However, like the California Essences which they resemble in scope and character, choice of the appropriate remedy relies on applied kinesiology or muscle testing, pendulum dowsing, other forms of divination and intuitive diagnosis. These methods of prescribing are very different from the close observation advocated by Bach, and although they have long been used in many forms of human and animal medicine, many owners, whose animals might benefit from treatment with flower essences, may feel uncomfortable about, and lack confidence in their use.

In Britain, the Bailey Flower Essences have been developed over a period of 20 years. This system comprises 36 essences produced using Bach's "sun" method of preparation. These are directed to treating unhealthy mental attitudes and stress and as such, it is claimed, have a direct relationship with the Bach remedies, which were developed for mental and emotional states. Although many of the descriptions provided in the repertory overlap with those given for Bach Flower Remedies, the essences are quite different, and while in principle it would seem that the essences might be suitable for animal use, there are no indications given for animals and no available literature documenting their use in animal treatment.

During the 1990s Doreen Paige added Celestial Remedies to her internationally recognized range of natural products for animals. These eight remedies, formulated by David Lovell, combine flower essences with gem elixirs and represent a further departure from the Bach system on which they are based.

Other systems of treatment with flower essences remain closer to that developed by Edward Bach. These include the Traditional Flower Remedies from Ellon, produced and distributed in the USA by Ralph and Leslie Kaslof, who on a large scale introduced Dr. Bach's flower preparations to America and were the exclusive distributor of them in the USA from 1979 to 1993. Since 1993, Ellon USA, now Global Health Alternatives, has been manufacturing homeopathically its own complete generic line of flower preparations discovered by Edward Bach from the same species of flowering plants, trees, and bushes as the original remedies under the trade name Ellon Traditional Flower Remedies.

In Britain Julian Barnard, who for some time was closely associated with the Bach Centre, and his wife Martine also maintain the tradition established by

Bach, preparing the same remedies as Bach in accordance with his original directions under the trade name of Healing Herbs. However, unlike the Bach Centre, which claims to use many of the flowers taken from the same sites as Bach in the development of his original system, they prepare their essences in their natural habitat, as do Global Health Alternatives in the USA. Therefore they are both unaffiliated with the Bach Centre, whose current custodians also refuse to recognize any remedies prepared in the tradition of Edward Bach other than those by the Bach Centre. As Mansfield (1995, p.16) points out:

> *The Bach Centre has naturally worked very hard to preserve the integrity and uniqueness of Dr. Bach's work and also to promote it throughout the world. In the process the scale of manufacture and the extent of the financial transactions involved have grown to such an extent that Dr. Bach might have found surprising. Naturally, running a business on such a scale has involved the occasional legal action to defend trade marks and copyrights, and also various attempts to control production of, and information concerning, the remedies. The business is now actually owned by Nelson's pharmacy and no doubt the additional support will enable further growth and development without compromising the quality of the remedies... This is a controversial matter: the "Bach purist" will stand by the letter of the doctor's statement that no more were needed, while those who are finding new remedies would say that the fact that they are being discovered shows the need at this time.*

Irrespective of either view, Bach Flower Remedies are certainly the best-known and most widely available system of healing with flower essences, and the most extensively used in the treatment of animals. For this reason, they form the basis of the Flower Essence Directory provided in Part II of this book.

# Chapter Two

# How Can Flower Essences Help Animals?

*They are so much more straightforward and honest. They have no sort of pretensions. They live out their lives in a special way – they know the rules and regulations. They live within their sphere of nature, they don't pretend they are God. They don't pretend they are intelligent, they don't invent nerve gas; and above all, they don't hold cocktail parties.*

*(Gerald Durrell, naturalist, conservationist and writer, on why he preferred animals to humans. The Ark's Anniversary, 1991).*

The principle underlying the use of flower essences in treatment is that states of mind are the primary cause of sickness and disease. Accordingly, personality and temperament are the major guide to their correct use. For some people this raises the question of their suitability for use in animals. In *The Descent of Man,* published in 1871, Charles Darwin insisted that "the senses, the various emotions and faculties such as love, memory, attention, curiosity, imitation, reason etc., of which man boasts, may be found in an incipient or even sometimes in a well-developed condition in the lower animals". He stressed that the higher animals and man share the same basic emotions and gave examples to show that some mammals at least are animated by more complex emotions such as shame, dislike of being laughed at, desire for deliberate revenge, and even a sense of humor. His views were at odds with the scientific thinking of his time, however, and they remain out of step with much current scientific opinion.

## INTELLIGENCE AND EMOTIONS IN ANIMALS

Stanley Coren, Professor of Psychology at the University of British Columbia, expert on canine intelligence and a prize-winning dog trainer, points out (1994) that until relatively recently there was a strong belief within the scientific community that animals are not conscious, thinking creatures with self-awareness and emotional feelings, but a bag of reflexes, automatic responses, and genetic programming, like biological machines. This view originates with the seventeenth-century French philosopher, René Descartes, who proposed that animals lack any sort of mind analogous to the human mind and are merely animate machines.

Pre-scientific peoples had no problems in attributing intelligence and emotions to animals, nor did early scientists. Most early scientific thinking followed that of the Greek philosopher Aristotle who claimed that there are several different qualities of life. The most basic are the ability to absorb food, move around in the environment, and reproduce. Higher abilities include perception of the world by way of the sense organs; capacity for emotions and motivations; intellectual capacity to learn, reason and analyze – all qualities of what are loosely termed *mind*. He believed that different creatures display more or less of each of these qualities, and that animals and humans differ only in the degree to which they possess certain mental abilities. Both have emotions, but human emotions are more complex; both learn, remember, solve problems, and benefit from experience, but humans are better at each of these.

Aristotle's view, that humans and animals differ only quantitatively in the degree to which their mental abilities express themselves rather than qualitatively in the nature of those mental processes, was established as a formal doctrine of the Church in the thirteenth century by St. Thomas Aquinas.

However, this subsequently led to complications. For some scholars in the Christian Church, accepting that animals possessed qualities then regarded as aspects of the soul was tantamount to conceding that they were candidates for an afterlife, including heaven. "A heaven occupied by such a collection of souls would fill to overflowing, and such an afterlife would not hold out adequate promise of a blissful existence to keep congregations on the straight and narrow path of virtue during their earthly years." (Coren 1994, p. 5–60) The existence of the animal soul also raised a whole series of ethical problems, such as whether animals should be killed for food, whether they should be denied free will by being forced into servitude, whether they should be granted access to the church and baptism. Philosophers of the time yielded to the power of the church, which controlled most research and scholarship, and being unable to acknowledge the possibility that animals had souls, for the sake of consistency they also denied them all other aspects of mind. Thus, "in order to prevent a population crisis in heaven and a philosophical problem on earth" (Coren, p.60), they had to reject the possibility that animals had intelligence, emotions, consciousness, and all other aspects of mind.

Descartes adopted this position wholeheartedly. He argued that animals are simply machines, and that the cry an animal releases when struck does not indicate pain but is the equivalent of the clanging of springs or chimes one might hear after dropping a clock or mechanical toy. The consequences for animals of his denial of their feelings and emotions were more than scientific and intellectual. It was subsequently used to justify massive and horrific cruelty to animals and the belief that moral concern about this is inappropriate since the pain and suffering of animals are not real. Some 350 years after Descartes, many people still subscribe to such views, including some psychologists and physiologists, and they can be found in scientific and philosophical literature, although they now appear less and less frequently.

However, as Coren points out, "It is interesting to note that scientists and philosophers with these views often act and believe quite differently in their personal lives" (p.65) Indeed, these extreme views are much more difficult to hold in private life, especially if one is living with a pet animal. Descartes himself owned a much pampered pet dog, worried about its health, likes, and dislikes, and often speculated about its thoughts. "Would one talk to a machine such as a wristwatch and speculate on its health and its likes?", asks Coren. (p.65)

Few people who live or work with animals doubt that they are affected by moods and emotions, which they express clearly and often in ways very similar to humans. Such was the view of Charles Darwin who drew attention to this similarity in his *The Expression of the Emotions in Man and Animals.* (1889) In this he dealt with the expression of the entire range of emotional states – joy, affection, pain, anger, fear, terror, grief, laughter, love, devotion, attention, and curiosity, including complex emotions or sentiments such as jealousy, sulkiness, disgust, astonishment, admiration, and shame. His own dog, Bob, provided excellent illustrations of many of these. Besides dogs and their wild relatives, he gave special attention to the emotional expressions of cats, horses, monkeys, and apes, but also included those of cattle and sheep, deer, elephants, rabbits, porcupines, hyenas, wild boars, kangaroos, a few birds, reptiles, and amphibians. The contemporary writer and veterinarian Richard Pitcairn (1983) reiterates Darwin's claims: "It is overwhelmingly true that animals have emotional states and feelings. If one is close to animals it can be seen clearly, yet it is not something that people ought to be convinced of intellectually. There is no question in my mind that animals experience the same range of emotions as people: love, fear, anger, grief, joy and so forth."

## PERSONALITY AND TEMPERAMENT IN ANIMALS

Similarly, few people who live and work with animals doubt that they have definite personalities and temperaments that are quite distinctive, and that no two animals, however closely related, are exactly alike, any more than two humans are. However, as Coren indicates, the term *personality* in relation to animals tends to be avoided by scientists and breeders alike because it is viewed as too mentalistic and implies characteristics that are human-like. Instead they use the term *temperament* which is considered more objective and neutral. This term was used by Clarence Pfaffenberger (1963), who was one of the most important figures in the development of selection and training programs for guide dogs for blind people. He was one of the first to suggest that considerations of a dog's personality are vital for certain working and obedience functions. He found that to be a good guide dog, an animal must have not only adequate intelligence but also an appropriate set of personality characteristics. While some traits allow dogs to apply their full adaptive intelligence in such a way that they become excellent working and obedience dogs, others prevent them achieving useful levels of functioning. Coren indicates that dog obedience instructors are only too well aware of what these characteristics are. The list includes:

> *(1) isn't interested in learning these sorts of things, (2) bores too easily, (3) is too independent, (4) has more important things on his mind, (5) doesn't get along well with other dogs (or people, noise, sunlight, walls or whatever), (6) is too easily distracted, (7) was bred to be a hunter (herder, guard, companion) not an obedience dog, (8) is too timid (or too dominant, too flighty, too laid-back, too happy-go-lucky, too depressed, too manic, too lazy, too dog-oriented, too people oriented, etc), (9) is a leader not a follower... the reasons are endless, and what they all come down to is that the dog is not unintelligent but rather has certain personality characteristics that interfere with its capacity to learn. (1994, p.189)*

Pfaffenberger therefore began breeding and selecting for both personality and intelligence, and by doing so he raised the percentage of dogs successfully completing the guide dog training program from 9% to 90%.

Many of the factors associated with personality are genetically determined, and people can breed for them in the same way as other characteristics. They are constitutional features. By keeping careful records, Pfaffenberger was able to show that many personality characteristics, including willingness to work for humans, are constitutional features. Since his initial work, others have become interested in assessing the personality of dogs, especially the specific character traits that make for good police dogs, hearing dogs, hospital visitation dogs, and so on. Jack and Wendy Volhard (Fisher & Volhard 1985) have developed a means of personality profiling designed to select dogs that match the lifestyle and needs of prospective owners, and this is becoming more widely known and used.

## ATTRIBUTING HUMAN CHARACTERISTICS TO ANIMALS

The personality traits of animals can be measured fairly objectively and reliably. The problem is, however, that on an ordinary day-to-day basis people are neither objective nor reliable in their observations and assessments of animals. They tend to project their own personality characteristics, feelings, thoughts, and moods on to them. This invariably obscures the true nature of the animal's behavior, sometimes with potentially dire consequences. For example, an elderly woman, Mrs. Gordon, claimed that Eddie, one of her daughter's pet sheep, "resented" her because he would push her with his head each time she bent over to collect eggs from a hen coup sited in his field. She had been pushed to the ground several times and on a couple of occasions she had been hurt. She resented the sheep for behaving in this way and was adamant that her daughter should "get rid" of this menace. As he was a castrated male, this would almost certainly mean that Eddie would be slaughtered.

Had Mrs Gordon observed the behavior of sheep more closely, she might have interpreted Eddie's action differently. He had been rejected by his mother at birth and bottle and bucket fed subsequently. Like all hand-reared sheep, he had learned to associate humans with food and to come running as soon as anyone entered his field, especially if they were carrying a bucket or other receptacle, as Mrs Gordon frequently did when collecting eggs. Anyone who has observed lambs feeding will have seen that they nudge the teats of ewes or bottles quite forcefully with their heads in order to express milk. Hand-reared lambs like Eddie also quickly learn that this tactic works equally well with buckets and that nudging them often results in the contents being spilled. Eddie therefore reacted to all humans in this way, not merely Mrs. Gordon, but being less strong than other members of the household, it was she who was most frequently unbalanced by his attention. It was therefore not so much a grudge he bore against her, as a nudge! The grudge was all hers. Fortunately for Eddie, Mrs. Gordon's daughter realized this and he was not despatched to the abattoir. Instead Mrs Gordon was "banned" from collecting eggs from his field.

Projecting human attributes on to animals may be amusing at times, but when we do so we no longer see them for what they are. Instead of seeing a sheep as a sheep or a horse as a horse, we see them as humans in different form. The behavior of cats, dogs, and other animals that live within the home is even more likely to be distorted through the projection on to them of human characteristics. Animal psychologist Robert Andrysko (1989) claims that "the hardest thing to convince an owner to do is to treat a dog like a dog". Indeed, research has shown that dog owners refer to their pets as a person more than cat owners. (Voith 1982, p.140)

Sometimes the behavior of animals resembles that of humans because that is how they make their wants and needs understood, but otherwise they are quite content to be themselves. The problem is that we are not content to let them, and no matter how kindly our intentions, these distortions can, and frequently do, lead to problems because they obscure the animal's true nature and its needs.

## THE HUMAN–ANIMAL BOND

Arguably, the main function of most pet animals is to meet human needs, and there is evidence that they meet numerous physical and psychological needs very effectively. Petting animals reduces anxiety and tension (Muschel 1984), blood pressure and heart rate (Baun et al. 1983; Friedman et al. 1983; Grossberg & Alf 1984; Jenkins 1984; Katcher 1981). Animal companionship makes us feel safer and more loved, increases our playfulness, allows us to express affection, increases our social interactions with others, and our level of exercise. The therapeutic benefit of companion animals is now widely recognized and is being made use of in a wide variety of institutional contexts. (Scarlett 1987; Whyte 1989)

Certainly people do use their pets to satisfy needs that are not met from more appropriate sources. Pelletier and Herzing (1989) observe that within Western culture kinship bonds and traditional family units are more difficult to cultivate, and some individuals supplement traditional support systems through relationships with animals. Animals provide companionship without the problems and demands of human communication, and acceptance without evaluation, so close and supportive relationships with animals often create strong and enduring bonds. The health benefits of these human–animal bonds have been reported for a variety of specific illnesses (Arehart-Treichel 1982; Holden 1981; Smith 1982) and in a number of medical and psychotherapeutic interventions (Arkow 1984; McCulloch 1982; Corson & O'Leary Corson 1979; Corson et al 1975, 1977; Mugford & McComisky 1975).

The human–animal bond may, however, be less healthy for animals. They may be used to satisfy human needs for relationship that are not satisfied in other ways and so treated as children, partners, or friends. Fogle (1986, p.18) points out that "the pet's symbolic role as a child is a self-evident one but pets can also act as symbolic adults. The well-trained guide dog for the blind is the classic example... but dogs can also act as adults in less obvious situations." Owners who regard their pets as children frequently admit to "spoiling" them, overindulging their whims and preferences, and this is frequently a cause of obesity and related health problems, as well as behavioral disorders.

Like children, companion animals may also copy their owners' temper tantrums and their other behavioral characteristics. Most animals taken as pets at a very young age become imprinted on humans. They live their lives in isolation from their own kind and identify instead with people. As animals rely largely on nonverbal communication, they tend to be better observers than humans, and they not only perceive and respond to, but also imitate, subtle human behaviors. They therefore tend to mirror their owners' mental and emotional states, both positive and negative – a phenomenon animal behaviorist Michael Fox (1985) refers to as "sympathetic resonance". The behavior of companion animals therefore largely reflects the human environment, and the attitudes and actions of their owners.

Certainly animals read the body language of humans far better than humans read that of animals. Owners generally are not aware of these behaviors and the extent to which animals mirror them. Moreover, as most owners are alienated from the real world of animals, they consider it normal for animals to act in human ways and wholly appropriate to attribute human qualities to them. Vets and animal behavior specialists are only too aware of this problem. Most would probably agree that at least 50% of their work involves treating owners, assessing to what extent the animal's problems have been introduced or encouraged by them, and educating them so that the animal doesn't get into the same state again.

Other owners may not treat animals as humans but as objects through which to satisfy needs for status or achievement. If the animals do not adequately meet these needs, they may be abandoned or discarded. Irrespective therefore of whether animals are treated as human or as objects, their true nature and their real needs tend to be obscured and distorted by human wants, and may be ignored or dismissed altogether, resulting in disorders and disease.

## FLOWER ESSENCES IN THE TREATMENT OF ANIMALS

Flower essences are important in the treatment of animals because they restore the balance and harmony of an animal's true nature, thereby remedying the disorders and diseases resulting from its distortion by humans. Their use requires careful, systematic, and objective observation of animal behavior and the situations in which it occurs rather than identification with, or interpretation of, it. Used properly, the dangers of interpreting animal behavior and emotions in human terms are avoided. In this way, an animal's true needs can be assessed and addressed.

Flower essences are safe to use alone or in conjunction with other forms of treatment, including allopathic or homeopathic medicines. Indeed, there are indications that flower essences act as a catalyst for homeopathic remedies and enhance their effects (Richardson-Boedler, 1994). They therefore have considerable appeal to those people, professional or lay, with an interest in the use of complementary medicine or adjuvant therapy. They are a totally natural, non-toxic product and do not produce the side effects and complications so frequently associated with the use of drugs and other pharmaceutical products. They also appeal to animal lovers because their production and development does not involve experimentation on live animals, as is the case with many orthodox drug and clinical treatments. Flower essences therefore provide a safe and gentle form of treatment. Moreover, "They're ridiculously inexpensive... What could be more gentle than that?" (Morrison 1995, p.128)

But do they work? Unlike homeopathic remedies, which have been extensively investigated in the treatment of animals, flower essences have not been subjected to little, if any, published controlled clinical trials. However, their use is becoming more widespread throughout the developed countries, especially among holistic and/or homeopathic veterinary practitioners and animal behavior therapists. As a result, there is abundant anecdotal evidence to suggest their effectiveness in animal treatment, much of it supplied by professionals in these fields. The information presented in Parts II and III of this book has been provided largely by veterinarians, animal behavior specialists, and therapists in interviews and correspondence with Gregory Vlamis or in scholarly publications and other published literature.

# PART II

# The Flower Essence Directory

The directory lists in alphabetical order 38 commonly available healing essences/remedies and the following details:

- the common name of the plant from which the essence derives.

- the botanical name of the particular variety from which the essence is taken.

- its mode of action (⊞), that is, the condition(s) it remedies and restores.

- behavioral indicators (🐾)for its use in various animal and bird species, most commonly domestic animals and pets such as parrots, cats, dogs, fish, horses, ponies, and rodents, but also, where applicable, wild and zoo animals, birds, and insects. This information draws principally on details and case material supplied to Gregory Vlamis in interviews with over 50 veterinarians, animal health, and behavior specialists in the UK and USA.

- other flower essences (✿) with which it can be combined.

- uses in humans (☺): possible uses for owners, handlers, and veterinarians, where appropriate.

# **A**GRIMONY *(Agrimonia eupatoria)*

Remedies mental or physical suffering or agony belied by outward appearances and behavior.

Restores inner peace and content.

- ☐ for animals that appear never to be quite at ease or relaxed, and whose owners describe them as appearing to "hold things in" or to "worry".
- ☐ for animals that appear normal except for a "pained" or anxious look in their eyes.
- ☐ for animals that never complain, even when they are clearly in pain.
- ☐ for animals anxious to please their owners all the time.
- ☐ for anxiety conditions that manifest in skin irritations, digestive upsets, urination or defecation.

## **Indications for use:**

🐾 Animals that conceal distress behind an apparently normal exterior, which make diagnosis difficult. Often the breathing pattern will provide an indication of the underlying distress. A pet animal may appear happy to see its owner, purring, or wagging its tail, but its tongue may hang out, or it may pant or drool and have excessive body heat. Its heart may be pounding and its paws sweating. When this pattern persists after the initial excitement has stopped, it indicates stress.

🐾 Animals in pain with dilated pupils to their eyes or a "pained expression". They may appear normal except for an exaggerated rise or roaching over the loin of the back caused by muscle tension. This typically occurs when they shift weight forward to take the strain off abdominal organs or the hindquarters.

🐾 **Birds** may show no signs of pain, illness or broken bones.

🐾 **Cats** that continue purring despite terminal conditions or irreparable fractures, or appear quite normal despite needles or thorns in their foot or injuries which their owners might consider agonizing. On picking up one of her cats, Helen felt a sharp prick seemingly from a very stiff hair on the skin on the animal's right foreleg. As this could be felt for several days, she became convinced the cat had a needle embedded in her leg and kept examining the protrusion. Eventually resorting to a pair of tweezers, she withdrew 1¹/₂ in. blackthorn that had penetrated the cat's leg from one side to the other. Although the thorn was as thick and sharp as a nail and had been embedded in the leg for some days, the cat at no time showed any discomfort or distress and purred throughout its removal. A human might suppose such an injury would be excruciating.

Owners tend to infer that animals are concealing their pain and "putting on a brave face" when in fact animals have a higher pain threshold and are less susceptible to psychological and emotional factors that contribute to the experience of pain than their human companions.

Some animals, particularly wild animals and birds, do conceal illness, indisposition, and wounds in order to avoid attack and elimination by other animals. Therefore some vets routinely administer Agrimony to establish the source of the pain. It is particularly useful in birds when pain or injury is suspected, and in wild animals that have been snared or trapped for some time.

🐾 **Cats** and **dogs** covering up distress by over-friendliness. Typically these animals cannot hold their focus or concentration. Many of them are stressed by their environment, particularly by domestic unrest: owners who argue with each other or who are undergoing marital difficulties. The animals therefore reflect domestic circumstances that their owners may be reluctant to reveal or admit.

Sometimes stress will show itself suddenly in strange behavior, such as defecation or urination on the owner's bed. Closer investigation of behavior patterns such as this may reveal a change in the animal's home environment.

Animals may also pick up anxiety from their owners or handlers. Outgoing dogs may bite heels or snap out of nervousness, and apparently happy cats may begin spraying in the house.

🐾 For some breeds of dog Agrimony may be a constitutional remedy (see page 99). Several vets associate it particularly with **Golden Retrievers** who often seem anxious to please their owners, and despite a constantly wagging tail, have a "shifty" look. **Boston Terriers** have also been identified as outgoing super-friendly dogs that are often unable to concentrate or hold focus.

🐾 **Dogs** with terminal conditions, notably cancers, and severe injuries, that continue wagging their tails, working, and playing. Their owners may be profoundly shocked when they realize how ill they are. Hilary Jupp (1990) suggests Agrimony as a constitutional remedy for **Irish Wolfhounds**, a breed typically stoical about suffering that manages to wag its tail and appear cheerful even when seriously ill. She recommends giving 6 drops to a gallon bucket of water.

🐾 **Horses** known to keep going despite X-ray evidence of widespread cancer of the leg. One such was George, a horse with cancer of the seismoid bone and little use of the affected leg. He showed no signs of suffering and his condition was only revealed when it became clear that despite his attempts he could no longer keep up with others. Agrimony was prescribed, together with Oak, the specific remedy for his constitutional type, Crab Apple to treat the disease itself, and Star of Bethlehem to remedy the shock to his system. After nine months' treatment with these remedies, he made a full recovery. The only evidence remaining of his illness was his x-ray plates and a slight thickening of the bone in the formerly affected leg.

🐾 Agrimony has proved effective in treating sick **golden hamsters**, which by nature are loners and relatively inexpressive animals.

☺ It may be useful for owners and vets undergoing stress they are reluctant to reveal or admit.

# ASPEN *(Populus tremula)*

Remedies fear and apprehension whose cause is unknown; sudden anxiety and nervousness as indicated by trembling, shaking, panting, snorting, sweating, urination, fearful look in the eyes, ears and tail down, cowering, and avoidance behaviors.

Restores calm and normal breathing; reduces muscle tension.

⊞ for animals that from birth have an obviously fearful and anxious character or constitution, and are typically "edgy", "jumpy", or "spooky".

+ for those that "freak out", becoming panicky, if presented with something new, unexpected, or different, or if they don't know what is going to happen next.

+ for animals that fear going outside.

+ for related physical conditions such as diarrhea, gastrointestinal problems, digestive disorders, bladder weakness, and circulatory problems, and in extreme cases, cardiac arrest and circulatory failure resulting from panic.

+ for animals that urinate through fear.

### Indications for use:

All animals difficult to house train or work because they refuse to go out of the house, stable, barn, or kennel, or are frightened of being outside. *Holistic Animal News* (Winter, 1986) reports the case of a normally outdoor six-year-old cat, frightened to go out for more than ten minutes once a week. Three hours after being given Aspen, he went in and out of the house several times and twenty-four hours later was back to normal.

**Cats** that overgroom, refuse to be handled, or are so timid their owners cannot get hold of them. One vet reports the case of a cat in an animal hospital being treated conventionally for cystitis. The cat was so timid its owners could not touch it, but after being given Aspen and Mimulus three times daily for two days while in the clinic, it would sit in laps. It continued to do so upon returning home, and its owners reported it to be a different animal.

Aspen may also be useful in the treatment of feline irritable bowel syndrome, together with Mimulus.

**Dogs** that whimper, shiver, cower, scurry back and forth, look fearful, hold their ears and tails down, bark at anything, hide behind or under furniture, back into corners, wriggle out of their collars, scratch at walls and doors in an attempt to get out. Effective in treating dogs that become panicky when their owners are packing or preparing to go out.

**Horses** that are highly strung, display shyness, refuse to go forward or pass things, pull away, rear up, refuse to be loaded into their boxes or trailers, or put in stalls.

🐾 Animals that behave strangely. In many animals, the fearful behavior may appear bizarre to the owner, such as when a cat leaps straight into the air upon entering a room for no apparent reason. This leads some owners to believe that their pets can see ghosts or spirits. Animals and birds can see, hear, and smell things humans cannot and are sensitive to changes in barometric pressure. They can therefore anticipate thunderstorms well before humans and can detect other events in advance, such as earthquakes. Some anticipate their owner's seizures. They can also pick up fears and anxieties from human companions and handlers, and fearful atmospheres in buildings. Their fears may therefore not be irrational or unfounded. For this reason Aspen is usually given in combination with Mimulus, the remedy for fear of known things.

Indeed, what starts as an unknown fear may become known, as in the case of a seven-year-old dog that suddenly and unaccountably became frightened of a wall in his owner's house. Upon finding that the neighbours had not made any changes to their side of the dividing wall, and that there were no new sounds there, the owner called in a priest to bless the house in a desperate and unsuccessful attempt to effect a cure. Subsequently it was realized that the "spooky" dog might have been frightened by the reflection of an exploding firework in a mirror hanging on that wall.

Animals with apparently strange behavior may also have received harsh treatment from previous owners or handlers. This is particularly true of animals that have spent time in shelters or rescue accommodation and sanctuaries. Animals that have spent time in shelters or kennels tend to cower and are generally fearful, should be given Aspen with Larch, the remedy for loss of confidence.

🐾 Animals experiencing changes in environment. Aspen may be used to good effect, in combinaton with Walnut, when animals are presented with new circumstances, such as when changing home, being placed in kennels or a cattery, when owners are away or pet sitters are called in.

☺ Animals with dominating owners. Owners who require an animal's submission at all times create constant anxiety. Animals overtaxed by their owners, that never know what the owner is going to demand of them next, often engage in submissive urination and other submissive, fearful behavior. In such cases Aspen is suitable for the animal and Vine, the remedy for dominance, ruthlessness, and inflexibility, is appropriate for the owner.

☺ It is also appropriate for anxious, nervous owners and handlers who may unwittingly communicate their fears to animals.

# BEECH *(Fagus sylvatica)*

Remedies intolerance.

Restores tolerance and flexibility.

⊞ for animals intolerant of change in routine.

⊞ for "touchy" animals that won't tolerate other animals near them or in the home.

⊞ for animals easily irritated and annoyed.

⊞ for tense, rigid animals that develop arthritic disorders as they get older.

⊞ for animals intolerant of sensory stimulation, oversensitive to sights, sounds, and touch, and with a low attention span.

⊞ for animals intolerant of climatic factors: heat, cold, humidity, rain, etc.

⊞ for animals intolerant of substances in the environment, that develop allergies, such as sensitivity to grasses.

## Indications for use:

🐾 **Birds** that peck intruders or strangers.

🐾 **Cats**, especially orientals such as **Siamese**, whose owners consider them arrogant; that swipe, bite, scratch, ambush, or turn their backs on people or other animals; adhere to a rigid routine and show annoyance when the owner doesn't come in or put food down at the right time; eat out of only one bowl; spray and become obnoxious when strange people or animals visit; sit rigidly and develop arthritic disorders. **Persian cats**, stressed by any change in routine, that urinate inconsistently and scratch destructively.

🐾 **Dogs** easily annoyed that show it by growling, raising their hackles, barking, biting, or attacking. Aggressive show dogs that cannot get on with other dogs in the show ring or at the ringside and object to being looked at or touched on the bench. Dogs upset by a change in routine, that must take their daily walks at the same time, for example.

🐾 **Horses** that bite; kick; rear up; back into people, other horses, and animals; object to being touched, saddled, shod, groomed, or mounted by other than their usual rider/owner; and object to visitors in their stalls, stables, travelling boxes, paddocks, etc.

🐾 Beech has proved effective in eradicating long-established stubborn behavior and also in promoting flexibility in tense horses, including dressage horses, that seem more rigid on one side than the other.

❀ Beech, Holly, Vine, and Willow all treat similar behaviors and a combination of all four is commonly used. Vine is indicated when the animal is clearly dominant and uses aggression to establish dominance over others and territory.

❀ Is useful, if used in combination with Rock Water, for horses that appear more rigid or tense on one side than the other.

🐾 Beech has proved effective in cases of spinal disc prolapse and subsequent paralysis in breeds prone to it such as **Dachshunds**. It lessens the danger of relapse by helping to reduce muscle tension and rigidity. It has also proved effective in the treatment of sensitivity and allergies.

☺ One vet admits to using Beech himself because of his reactions to some clients!

☺ Beech may also be effective for intolerant owners and those who feel that their partner's pet gets more attention than they do.

# CENTAURY *(Centaurium umbellatum)*

Remedies lack of assertiveness, servility, and weak will.

Restores assertiveness, individuality, and resistance.

+ for animals (more commonly females) so insecure and overanxious to please that they may become obnoxious, following their owners around all the time, licking them constantly, and refusing to leave them alone.

+ for "doormats" – animals that are too submissive and subordinate and as a result are easily exploited, imposed upon, tired, and worn out. They will often lower their head, avoid eye contact with others, and keep the ears pressed back and close to the head; adopt characteristic submissive postures, hugging the ground, exposing their throats and under-bellies. They may also show submission by urinating. Unable to stand up for themselves, these animals are often bullied by other animals or humans, especially children, and deprived of their food and toys.

+ for animals who become overtired from being overworked or overtaxed.

+ for animals that are very weak after illness.

+ for those with no resistance to the environment, that catch infections and parasites easily, and through lack of stability tend to react intensely to feeding mistakes.

+ for additional therapy during convalescence following acute illnesses or accidents.

## Indications for use:

🐾 All animals subject to bullying.

🐾 **Birds** low in the peck order that have suffered stress or injury, to help them stand up for themselves.

🐾 **Dogs** that don't grow out of normal puppy submissiveness; those such as **Labradors, Collies** and **Cavalier King Charles Spaniels** that will chase a ball for hours on end; and hunting dogs that carry on until they drop.

🐾 **Horses**, especially hunters, and eventers that will go on forever.

🐾 **Ponies** bullied by the herd. One week after being treated with Centaury and Larch, one badly bullied pony was reported as standing and eating with the herd, and two months later was noticeably higher in the hierarchy than previously.

🐾 All animals during acute illnesses, convalescence following accidents, or long-term debilitating conditions, especially liver disease; that do not eat well for some time, become thin, and prone to stomach upsets.

✿ Olive combines well with Centaury as a strengthener for animals very weak after illness, and with Oak where endurance is a factor in the animal's weakness.

☺ Animals needing Centaury sometimes have strong-willed or abusive owners, who may view the Centaury type as the ideal kind of dog. Vine may help remedy the owner's behavior, but if it does not, the animal will derive limited benefit from Centaury.

# CERATO *(Ceratostigma willmottiana)*

Remedies lack of self-assurance and confidence, lack of initiative, approval seeking from others, imitative behavior.

Restores self-assurance, confidence, and initiative.

⊞ for animals that are totally dependent on human caretakers, looking to them to know what to do and how to respond, and cannot act on their own initiative; for animals that when given a command, look to others for the appropriate responses; and for "copy cats" that imitate the behavior of others.

⊞ for animals during competitive show events to assure the animal's ability to be undistracted and to listen to the handler's commands.

⊞ for animals that cannot relate to members of their own species, have inadequate social behavior, and difficulties engaging in mating behavior.

⊞ for animals that remain juvenile in behavior.

⊞ for animals whose lack of confidence is a general characteristic rather than a specific loss of confidence (the remedy for which is Larch).

## Indications for use:

🐾 All animals and birds deprived of same species contact. It helps them to adjust when presented with members of their own species.

🐾 **Birds**, especially **parrots**, that develop severe behavioral problems and reproductive difficulties in the absence of other members of their own species.

🐾 **Dogs** that "go to pieces" in the show ring when required to be handled or moved individually; working trial dogs that can't work when out of the handler's sight; would-be police and guide dogs that cannot work independently and would otherwise be discarded; hunting dogs that need to show initiative; dogs such as sled dogs trained as a team; and stud dogs who look to their owner for approval before mounting and mating bitches.

🐾 **Horses**, used for hunting, eventing, and showjumping, and polo **ponies** that need to take initiative rather than rely solely on the rider; and those that rely too much on one rider.

🐾 Herd animals, easily influenced by others, that develop bad habits and follow the wrong animal.

☺ Cerato is useful for owners who doubt their own intuition and judgment regarding the health and well-being of their animals, or in relation to euthanasia, who constantly seek the advice of veterinarians and others despite sometimes feeling foolish in doing so, or who follow advice from others even when they doubt its usefulness. As having no leader often produces the Cerato state in animals, the owner's attitude can contribute to an animal's uncertainty. Where this is the case, Cerato is recommended for both animal and owner.

# CHERRY PLUM (Prunus cerasifera)

Remedies uncontrollable behavior, craziness, compulsiveness.

Restores calmness and control.

⊞ for basically nervous animals that become hysterical, go berserk, go into an uncontrollable rage or frenzy, or into total panic through fear, endangering themselves or others.

⊞ for unpredictable animals that respond to fright with an extreme fight/flight reaction, attack, or become nasty, or desperately try to get out of whatever situation they are in, crashing through windows and destroying doors, walls, trailers, cars, etc.

⊞ for animals whose destructive behavior is aggravated by red dyes and other food additives.

⊞ for self-destructive behavior such as biting and tearing at the skin and excessive licking.

⊞ for uncontrollable urination, loss of control of bodily functions.

⊞ for animal mothers that destroy their young at birth.

⊞ for recurrent phobias.

⊞ for animals that suffer psychomotor seizures, epilepsy, or fits.

## Indications for use:

🐾 All animals in extreme distress or whose extreme behavior causes their owners to be afraid of them and/or to consider euthanasia; those "driven crazy" by parasitic infections or ear mites.

🐾 **Birds** in a frenzied state (Cherry Plum can be sprayed on to their feathers).

🐾 **Dogs** whose apparently self-destructive behavior is often described by owners as "suicidal"; that destroy furniture, mattresses, carpets, curtains; become frantic at the prospect of having their nails clipped or their teeth cleaned; "freak out" in the show ring or in the veterinary clinic. It may be used as a constitutional remedy to treat the "rage syndrome" in golden and red **Cocker Spaniels**. In some cases it has eliminated the need for the animal to be put down.

🐾 **Horses** that buck, kick, bite, rear, bolt, and try to kick out of stables or trailers; that go wild when saddled or mounted. High-performance animals such as **racehorses** when passed on to new homes and uncontrolled.

♣☺ Cherry Plum is rarely used alone. The animal's extreme behavior may be the owner's fault, the result of bad handling or previous abuse, where it has been pushed to extremes physically or emotionally. It is therefore usually given in conjunction with Aspen, the remedy for unknown fears. As owners are usually afraid of the animal's behavior and may have caused it by their own behavior, Cherry Plum is recommended for both animal and owner.

✿ However, it is often not used in the first instance. Most vets use Rescue Remedy or other equivalent composite remedies (see Emergency Remedies page 87) of which Cherry Plum is a component.

# CHESTNUT BUD *(Aesculus hippocastanum)*

Remedies failure to learn from experience, repetition of the same mistakes, and repetitive behavior.

Restores the ability to learn and utilize experiences.

⊞ for any kind of repetition where an animal seems unable to learn from experience, repeating the same mistakes and the same patterns of behavior.

⊞ to break bad habits.

⊞ for accident-prone animals.

⊞ for recurrent sicknesses and fungal infections that resist other treatment methods.

⊞ for repeated birth difficulties and for animal mothers that repeat behaviors such as eating, crushing, or rejecting their offspring.

## Indications for use:

🐾 **Cats** that repeatedly urinate in the house or outside the litter tray; scratch furniture.

🐾 **Dogs** difficult to house or lead train; that repeat mistakes in training; fail obedience tests; make the same mistakes time and again in the show ring or in working trials; continue to chase cars after being hit by one; have painful encounters with porcupines and still go back to them; persist in emptying the dustbin or garbage pail despite punishment;

chew shoes; chase horses, cats, chickens; farm dogs that eat chicken eggs and/or kill chickens.

🐾 **Horses** that won't listen to or respond to commands; keep hitting the same fences and making the same mistakes when eventing or in dressage; repeatedly get caught in barbed wire or electric fences.

🐾 **Sheep** that repeatedly leap or push under fences or become ensnared in them.

✿ Use in combination with Rock Water to aid learning and limit repetitive behavior.

☺ Chestnut Bud is particularly appropriate for owners who consistently fail to observe animals and their needs, and those who repeat the same mistakes in training an animal, for example by using the wrong commands or punishing it for making a mess in ways that increase its anxiety and its tendency to make such a mistake. One such owner complained to her vet that her dog kept making a mess indoors in spite of how many times she hit it when she came in. She seemed unable to accept that the dog's anxiety about being hit when she returned home was at the root of its problem.

# CHICORY *(Chicorium intybus)*

Remedies possessiveness, clinging behavior, and attention seeking.

Restores normal protectiveness and caring.

⊞ for animals that won't let their owner out of sight; sulk when they can't get their own way; become destructive, dirty, or noisy when their owners leave them; bark, bite, limp, or vomit to prevent them leaving.

⊞ for attention-seeking behavior and animals that won't allow others to gain any attention.

⊞ for overprotective animals.

⊞ for animal mothers that don't wean their offspring and continue to nurse and lick them after they are weaned.

**Indications for use:**

- **Birds** that sulk when they don't get their own way. Chicory has been successfully used on a swan that became overdependent on humans following the death of its mate.

- **Cats** that follow their owners everywhere, want to sit on them all the time or literally cling to their owners. Some vets describe them coming into their surgeries clinging to the owner's shoulders, going berserk when placed on the examining table and returning immediately to the owner's shoulder. Chicory has been used successfully to prevent a Siamese cat seeking attention by climbing up curtains. It can also be used for those that bite or nip to gain attention.

- **Dogs** that follow owners everywhere, even to the bathroom; guard dogs such as **Rottweilers, Dobermans, German Shepherds** whose natural protectiveness is exaggerated; dogs that nip or bark, grab curtains or pull sheets off the bed for attention; and those that suffer separation anxiety. In some cases dogs exhibit physiological responses such as vomiting, diarrhea, increased heart rate or respiration, or self-injurious behaviors such as hair chewing, pulling out hair, or excessive licking of the body, when separated from the owner. In such cases Chicory can be combined with Rescue Remedy and White Chestnut for repetitive, obsessive behavior.

- **Horses** that have grown too attached to stable mates and call to them when separated; mares overprotective of foals that keep owners and other horses away with bare teeth and hooves.

- ☺ Frequently there is a co-dependent relationship between the animal and its owner. The owner who displays Chicory behavior often encourages it in the animal, and so Chicory is suitable for both.

# CLEMATIS *(Clematis vitalba)*

Remedies absentmindedness, lack of interest in present circumstances.

Restores alertness and focus.

- ⊞ for inattentive animals lacking concentration.

+ for animals that look dazed or have a vacant "spacy" expression as if they're not all there.

+ for bored animals.

+ for disinterested, unresponsive, dull, lazy animals that sleep a good deal.

+ for shock when the body feels cold to the touch.

+ after collapse through exhaustion, loss of consciousness, coma, fainting, concussion, epileptic fits.

+ after surgery to assist waking, prevent drowsiness and listlessness, and to aid recovery.

+ for revitalization of prematurely aged animals with memory dysfunctions or senility.

**Indications for use:**

**Birds** stunned by flying into windows (give every five minutes).

**Cats** with a vacant expression may be regarded as abnormal when in fact "day-dreaming" is quite normal behavior. However, cats do not normally fall off window ledges through lack of alertness, especially when the window is that of a fifth floor apartment. One that did just that benefited from Clematis.

**Dogs** difficult to train (can be combined with Chestnut Bud).

**Horses** unable to focus attention on their handlers; whose attention is difficult to gain.

# CRAB APPLE (Malus pumila)

Remedies uncleanliness, infection, toxicity.

Restores cleanliness and dignity.

+ for fastidious creatures suffering diarrhea, incontinence, kidney disease.

+ for animals caged or confined with their own excrement and urine.

+ for involuntary defecation or incontinence during illness or seizures.

+ for constipation.

+ for obsessive grooming.

+ for all skin conditions where animals are always cleaning themselves, licking, scratching, or pulling hair out.

+ for acute and chronic skin problems, abscesses, acne, eczema, dermatitis, dandruff, lick sores and granulomas, mange, scabies, scale, tartar.

+ for animals with fleas, parasites, ticks, insect bites, or that tend to attract fleas and parasites.

+ for worm infestation.

+ for animals with hair loss despite a coat in otherwise good condition.

+ for animals with heavily matted coats.

+ for any dietary change.

+ to assist weight loss in diabetic animals.

+ during fasting.

+ for animals that eat the dung of others (coprophagia).

+ for the elimination of toxins in animals that have been poisoned, have licked near insecticides or antifreeze, or are suffering from liver disease.

+ for animals that express the need for inner cleansing by going off their food and seeking out grass and herbs to eat.

+ for allergies.

+ for cleaning abscesses and wounds.

+ for all sick animals as a detoxifier and cleanser.

+ for use in conjunction with conventional treatment, particularly long-term courses of antibiotics or steroids, and in adrenal disorders where strong medication may have adverse effects.

+ for preventive use where there is a danger of infection, and before surgery.

+ for obstructions in the gut such as bone splinters and fur balls.

+ for withdrawal of foreign bodies such as parasites, splinters, stones, dirt, from the eyes and skin.

## Indications for use:

🐾 All animals that are incontinent and/or badly matted and show distress at their condition.

🐾 **Cats**, especially elderly cats or those with arthritis of the spine, that are unable to groom themselves and become depressed and miserable; those that overgroom; male cats suffering from Stud Tail, a disease of the sebaceous glands along the top of the tail and base of the spine caused by blockage of the glands with fluid.

🐾✿ **Dogs** whose coats have become badly matted, especially long-haired dogs such as **Afghan Hounds, Bearded Collies, Old English Sheepdogs, Poodles, Lhasa Apsos,** and **Shih Tzus;** dogs that lick or chew their feet, lick frantically, have running eyes, ears, noses; that have anal gland infection, wind, irregular motions, drink a lot of water; that suffer from degenerative myopathy, spondylitis (an arthritic condition of the spine), or hip dysplasia – conditions that interfere with nerve function and may lead to loss of bowel control. Where the dog scratches persistently or licks repetitively, Crab Apple should be combined with White Chestnut.

🐾 **Dogs** with mange. Jon Tuxworth (1981) reports that the worst case of follicular mange he had ever seen was successfully treated by Crab Apple. The whole body of this **Skye Terrier** "was covered with pustules, the skin was a leathery grey and the hair falling out in huge patches. The dog was in a hypersensitive state and obviously felt very uncomfortable with his body". Crab Apple was prescribed externally to cleanse his body and to rid him of the feeling of uncleanness, together with Vervain for his highly-strung state and the surface irritation. Crab Apple dabbed on externally helped to draw out the parasites thriving in the serum-filled pustules.

🐾 **Goats** with scab.

🐾✿ **Horses** with itchiness, insect bites. Tuxworth (1981) reports that Queensland Itch – a skin allergy caused by mite bites, and similar to flea allergy in dogs – responds to Crab Apple and Rescue Remedy Cream (see page 91), which contains Crab Apple.

🐾 **Sheep** with ticks, sheep scab.

🐾 Crab Apple has been successfully used to treat a hedgehog, one of whose legs was in an advanced state of decomposition and virtually missing. After three weeks the leg had regenerated and the bone had grown.

❀ Combine with Water Violet for removal of foreign bodies in the eyes, ears, or skin.

> **Caution:** Veterinary advice should be sought for all disorders of defecation and urination. Scabies, or sarcoptic mange, is highly infectious to animals and humans. Veterinary attention should be sought in all suspected cases and rubber gloves worn when handling affected animal.

**Administration:** Crab Apple can be given orally, in baths and sprays or in cream. It is an ingredient in Rescue Remedy (see page 87) which can be applied topically.

# Elm *(Ulmus procera)*

Remedies inadequacy.

Restores competence, efficiency, and resistance.

⊞ for animals overwhelmed by a situation, work, or training when too much is asked of them resulting in temporary exhaustion, "burn out", or withdrawal not normal for them.

⊞ where an animal has difficulty adjusting to the demands of a more active life or a more demanding owner.

⊞ for animal mothers overwhelmed by the demands of their offspring, especially where there are multiple births or large litters.

⊞ during birth to regularize contractions and prevent overstrain.

⊞ for animals overwhelmed by illness.

⊞ for animals that develop stress allergies.

⊞ for animals that develop the same disorders as their owners.

## Indications for use:

🐾 All animals in competition that are on the circuit every weekend, or 2-3 times a week; working despite decreased vision or hearing, or with arthritis; geriatric animals in households where children are introduced.

🐾 **Cats** required to share a litter tray with several others.

🐾 **Dogs** whose owners train them like robots, or every day, and follow a rigid routine; all working dogs, especially mountain rescue animals, drug search dogs, police, army, and bomb squad dogs; guide and hearing dogs; racing and coursing dogs. Elm has been used effectively to treat a guide dog whose owner suffered a heart attack in the street (the dog tried to protect its owner by keeping at bay those people trying to help, and afterwards would not allow himself to be harnessed); also to treat a police dog becoming deaf in one ear and more and more gun shy.

🐾 **Hamsters** that are overactive by night in treadwheels.

🐾 **Horses** used by mentally handicapped and disabled riders, especially riders suffering spasms; racehorses; police horses used for crowd control; and those that overextend themselves.

❀ Elm can be used with Oak, the remedy for endurance, and Larch, the remedy for loss of confidence

☺ It may be of benefit to animal owners and handlers because often the animal takes on the problems of the owners or the household, especially where the animal is dominant and regards the family as its pack; and for vets who feel overwhelmed by clients, especially clients requiring emotional support when their companion animal is suffering a lingering illness, or following euthanasia.

# GENTIAN *(Gentiana amarella)*

Remedies easy discouragement, despondency, weakness after illness, lack of interest in food.

Restores perseverance and appetite.

- ⊞ for animals that become discouraged, give up, and stop eating, especially when ill or following loss of owner or of a companion animal with which they have grown up.

- ⊞ for animals that become despondent following domestic upheaval.

- ⊞ for animals in rescue shelters, kennels, or catteries, especially those caged after living in a house, that become listless, sleep much of the time, and whose coat is dull. In such cases also consider Wild Rose.

- ⊞ for animals not praised or encouraged by their handlers during training, performance, or competition.

- ⊞ for animals that suffer a setback or relapse when ill.

- ⊞ ✿ for animals that won't eat when given medication, or when suffering congestive heart failure. Use in combination with Gorse, the remedy for hopelessness.

- ⊞ for animals that, in the absence of physical injury, lose form and can't regain it.

- ⊞ for recovery from orthopedic injury and orthopedic correction, in conjunction with Oak and Larch.

## Indications for use:

- 🐾 All animals who refuse to eat.

- 🐾 **Cats** that suffer stress when in catteries and refuse to eat; those (typically **Siamese**) that give up when ill; suffer relapses with feline leukemia, or suffer a setback following hysterectomy.

- 🐾 ✿ **Dogs**, especially **Collies**, that give up when sick; suffer setback following hysterectomy; experience setback during training (in combination with Chestnut Bud).

- 🐾 **Horses**, especially eventers, that cannot regain form despite absence of physical injury; those that cannot make a jump; and horses kept alone without companions.

✿ Gentian is often used with Gorse, which reinforces its tonic effects, and with Chestnut Bud when animals become discouraged during training.

☺ It may benefit owners who become disappointed or discouraged by an animal's performance during training or competition, when an animal's condition worsens and/or when they are discouraged about an animal's prospects for recovery.

# GORSE *(Ulex europaeus)*

Remedies utter despondency and hopelessness.

Restores perseverance, endurance, and vitality.

⊞ for animals that appear to have lost heart and given up; that show great lethargy, apathy, low energy when ill or in confinement.

⊞ for animal mothers that lose their offspring.

⊞ for animals that don't respond to encouragement.

## Indications for use:

🐾 **Birds** shot through the wing.

🐾 **Cats**, especially orientals, that give up when ill.

🐾 **Dogs** that remain for long periods in rescue kennels and pounds; obese animals that show great lethargy.

🐾 **Horses** suffering from laminitis, a painful condition of the feet that may prevent them sleeping.

☺ Gorse is indicated where symptoms are more extreme than those for which Gentian is appropriate, that is, for hopelessness rather than despondency and for lack of response. Gorse works synergistically to reinforce the effects of Gentian in the treatment of cancer and leukemia, and in cases of relapse. It may be a useful remedy for owners whose animals are suffering terminal conditions.

# HEATHER (Calluna vulgaris)

Remedies noisy attention-seeking and loneliness.

Restores composure.

+ for animals that crave attention, are noisy, obtrusive, destructive, or dirty when left alone.

+ for animals that are inattentive to the commands of owners and handlers.

## Indications for use:

- All animals that drain their owner's energy by constantly demanding attention.

- **Birds**, especially **parrots, cockatiels, mynah birds**, and **macaws** that will not be quiet.

- **Horses** that when left alone pace and bang into the stable walls; that won't listen to commands from their riders.

- **Cats** that always purr and miaow for attention, and are constantly "in the face" of their human companions.

- **Dogs** that bark, yap, whine or howl excessively, groan and otherwise complain when ill, and won't do as they are told because they don't listen to their owners.

Fogle (1986, p.35) observes that "pet owners interpret their dog's attachment to them in their own idealistic ways. And the more intensely both the pets and their owners feel about attachment, the more varied will be the separation games that they play." In the annual report (1994) of The Association of Pet Behaviour Counsellors (APBC), separation problems are cited as the third most commonly presented behavioral problem in dogs. These problems, owing mainly to over-attachment, include destructive behavior such as biting doors and door frames in an attempt to follow the owner, loss of toilet control because of anxiety at being left alone, and excessive barking to call the owners home. These types of problems are more frequent in bitches than male dogs and peak in January, May, and August following Christmas, Easter, and summer holidays when families have spent prolonged periods of time with their dogs.

Dogs that were the single, or solo, puppy in a litter and received exclusive attention from their dam and from humans early in life tend to grow up to be attention seekers that want to be the center of attention at all times. (Graham 1993)

❀ Heather has an excellent synergistic effect with Chicory.

☺ It may be useful for owners who won't listen to the advice of vets, obedience trainers, handlers, and riders.

# Holly *(Ilex aquifolium)*

Remedies suspiciousness, maliciousness, and revenge.

Restores tolerance.

⊞ for "prickly" animals that react intensely to loss of status or attention with viciousness, suspicion, defiance, bad temper.

⊞ for animals discontent with the treatment they receive from their owner.

⊞ for animals with very specific hates or dislikes, such as cats, vets. postmen.

⊞ for pack animals that don't get on well together.

⊞ for intense illnesses; highly acute, very severe allergies; urticaria; asthma attacks; sudden high fevers ("raging conditions"); severe pains and infections.

## Indications for use:

🐾 All animals that are "prickly" or bad-tempered when there is uncertainty about the appropriate remedy.

🐾 **Dogs** with bad temperament that growl and bite owners or their children; hate cats, vets, postmen, etc; pack or kennel dogs that fight; and bitches that can't get along together.

🐾 **Horses** that bite and kick, are difficult to stable, and don't want to be touched.

✿☺ Holly combines well with Beech and is helpful when introducing a new baby or animal into an environment. It may also be useful for owners angry at their vet when euthanasia is called for, or with drivers responsible for the injury or death of their animals in road traffic accidents.

# Honeysuckle *(Lonicera caprifolium)*

Remedies homesickness and difficulty in adjusting to new circumstances.

Restores adjustment to present circumstances.

⊞ for animals that pine or become depressed, ill, feeble, or thin when away from home.

⊞ for animals that dislike being on holiday with their owners.

⊞ for animals that pine when boarded.

⊞ for lost or rescued animals that can't adjust to new accommodation and/or owners.

⊞ for animals that keep returning to former homes.

⊞ for animals that pine for former owners, dead owners or companions, children that have gone away to school.

⊞ for the revitalization of old animals.

⊞ for re-establishment of newly achieved health after severe sickness and for the prevention of relapses.

## Indications for use:

🕷 All animals that need a new home because of their owner's death; that get lost and taken into new homes or sanctuaries; are rescued and re-homed; or whose history is unknown.

🕷 **Cats** that lose hair and develop skin disorders when pining for former homes, owners, and companions; that return to previous homes; that are confined indoors after having had access to outdoors; that sit at the window looking for owner or waiting for doors to open.

- **Dogs** (like "Greyfriars Bobby") that sit by the graves of dead owners and won't leave; like the Akita that used to escort his owner home every night from the railway station after work and continued to visit the station every morning and evening for the rest of its life after the owner, who had been killed at work, failed to return; those that wait at doors or windows all day waiting for their owners to return; dogs, especially bitches, that won't eat or eliminate when away from home; puppies going into new homes.

- **Ponies** that are passed on and miss their former owners and families.

☺ Honeysuckle is recommended for owners who constantly make unfavourable comparisons between an animal and a previous one.

❁ It can be combined with Walnut to help animals adjust to changes of home or owner.

❁ It can be combined with Rock Water as an aid to promoting adjustment and adaptability.

# **H**ORNBEAM *(Carpinus betulus)*

Remedies weakness, inability to cope because of tiredness and weariness.

Restores vitality.

+ for animals lacking "get up and go" when they are required to perform following a period of inactivity.

+ for animals during periods of enforced inactivity.

+ for animals needing a "pick me up" after illness.

+ for animals with illnesses whose symptoms are worst in the morning but improve during the day.

+ for the day-to-day treatment of animals suffering from cancer.

## Indications for use:

- All animals subjected to a change of routine on a weekly basis, such as owners returning to work or school on Monday mornings, especially when most of the animal's activity is packed into the weekend; after holidays or periods of leave; animals in competition on successive days; those that have been through a taxing ordeal or illness.

- **Dogs** for whom readjustment on Monday mornings when their owners return to work is difficult; working dogs, such as police and army dogs, after long periods of work; those obliged to accompany owners when they run or jog several miles; those recovering from parvovirus and other debilitating diseases.

- **Horses** alone all week after being worked at the weekend; that won't eat on Monday mornings; racehorses "let down" after hard work.

- Hornbeam combined with Olive is recommended when animals are tired and lethargic, especially if the reason for the listlessness is uncertain.

---

**Caution:** Listlessness may be a symptom of illness and owners should consult a vet if it persists for several days. In female dogs listlessness may be the first sign of womb disease such as pyometra, especially if the animal is also off its food and drinking more than usual. In such cases delay can prove fatal and therefore veterinary attention should be obtained as soon as possible.

---

# IMPATIENS (Impatiens glandulifera)

Remedies impatience, irritability, lack of co-operation.

Restores patience, calm, and co-operation.

- [+] for excitable animals in training that seem in too much hurry to learn and make mistakes through rushing.

- [+] for animals that can't wait to go out, get in, get off the lead, eat, drink, etc.

- [+] for impatient team animals.

- for hyperactive, restless animals that can't gain or maintain weight, or that lose weight easily.

- for animals that become restless if given insufficient occupation or attention.

- for the relief of tension in edgy, "uptight", quick animals requiring treatment.

- for the relief of muscular cramp.

- for skin irritations, itching, eczema.

- for irritable bowel syndrome, indigestion, gastrointestinal problems, colic, vomiting and diarrhea seemingly unrelated to diet.

- for the treatment of pain (muscle tension increases pain).

## Indications for use:

**Birds**, especially **parrots**, that are irritable.

**Dogs** that are hyperactive and excitable during obedience or show training; show dogs that fidget and don't co-operate with their handlers; **greyhounds** "uptight" before races; herding dogs that become excited if herd animals don't move quickly enough and bite their heels; sled dogs that become impatient when others won't keep up. "Pushy" dogs that jump up and knock things over. Impatiens has also been used to good effect in stabilising breathing difficulties in **Pekinese.**

Tuxworth (1981) describes the successful use of Impatiens as follows:

*A friend who runs weekend obedience classes asked for my advice concerning a young puppy who was disrupting her training sessions. He was an eight-month old Labrador, beautifully bred, intelligent, but very boisterous and always wanting to leap ahead of the others in his group. Impatiens was prescribed as his type remedy to restrain his exuberance and Chestnut Bud to help him learn the important lesson of discipline and save him from repetitive mistakes. At the class the following Sunday, the transformation was amazing – a different puppy sat alertly and quietly beside his young mistress. Eagerly, he went through his paces but without his former impetuosity and in no time was ready to graduate from the beginner's class – fulfilling the promise the instructor had seen in the dog from the outset.*

- **Horses** that don't like being touched; are difficult to saddle because they won't stand still or be restrained; rush their fences and make mistakes; racehorses that break into a gallop on the way to the starting line; team horses impatient with others that don't keep up. Impatiens has also been used successfully to free movement in arthritic horses.

- **Mules** that won't co-operate with others in teams.

- **Wild animals** tense and uptight when in captivity or when trapped in snares.

☺ Impatiens is also suitable for owners and handlers who want immediate results and for vets who become impatient with owners that keep asking the same questions and cannot decide on the treatment option or on euthanasia.

**Caution:** Irritability in animals may result from pain. It may be that animals that become increasingly irritable over time are suffering chronic pain such as arthritis, hip dysplasia, other musculoskeletal, degenerative diseases, or cancer. Impatiens can help to reduce or remove pain by relieving muscle tension, but it will not necessarily remedy the underlying physical condition which can only be established by veterinary examination.

# LARCH (Larix decidua)

Remedies loss of confidence, hesitancy, fear of failure.

Restores confidence and willingness to try.

+ for any situation where an animal's confidence has been compromised.

+ for animals that have been abused or traumatized at some time.

+ for easily intimidated animals.

+ for animals that need coaxing.

+ for animals with poor resistance to illness.

## Indications for use:

🌸 All animals entering rescue shelters, and whose owners or handlers have been or are heavy-handed; animals that have been ill for some time and have lost their former standing with companions.

🌸 **Cats** inferior in households where one animal is very dominant; animals that begin to spray; cats that won't try new foods; adopted strays.

🌸 **Dogs** in competition that lose confidence in themselves and/or their handlers; that have been wrongly taught by their owners and become confused when taken to obedience/training classes; that surrender to others; and puppies.

🌸 **Horses** that lack confidence in their riders; who fall at fences or won't attempt them.

☺ Larch is useful for owners, handlers and riders who lack confidence, are diffident in their performance, or will not try to handle or train their animals because they fear failure.

# Mimulus (Mimulus guttatus)

Remedies fear of known things, shyness, timidity.

Restores courage.

⊞ for animals that fear cold, dark, water, pain, telephones, traffic, thunderstorms, vacuum cleaners, stairs, bridges, baths, cars, trailers, radios, airplanes, guns, fireworks, flags, confined spaces, other animals, men, vets, people in white coats, being groomed, being clipped, having nails clipped, etc; that fear insects following a severe stinging; the smell of burning following experience of a fire.

⊞ for animals that show their nervousness by restlessness, pacing, rushing to and fro, frothing at the mouth, whining, laying their ears back, shivering, snorting, flaring their nostrils, puffing, blowing, panting, sweating, unsteadiness, rigidity, etc.

⊞ for the treatment of heart disorders.

## Indications for use:

- All animals reacting fearfully to people, other animals, objects, noises, or specific circumstances.

- **Cats** afraid of travelling in cars.

- ✿ **Dogs**, especially bitches, very commonly develop phobias. As they tend to generalize fear to other things, fearful animals may have several phobias, or develop new phobias when others appear to have been successfully overcome. Extreme fear is most commonly associated with thunderstorms and fireworks. Mimulus combines well with Rock Rose to treat dogs normally terrified on Bonfire Night, Independence Day and Halloween. Dogs may also fear travelling in motor vehicles, on trains and in airplanes. Mimulus gives extra courage to show dogs, can be used to treat greyhounds frightened of starting traps, and fear-biters, who bite out of fear rather than aggression.

- **Horses** afraid of the dark, shadows, dogs, saddles, whips, gates, etc; of being shod or clipped; of travelling, crossing bridges, or passing openings in hedges, gateways etc; racehorses frightened of traps, starter gates, and pistols; and for those with nervous riders.

- ☺ Mimulus can be used for adults and children fearful of animals or specific kinds of animal; nervous riders and handlers.

# Mustard *(Sinapsis arvensis)*

Remedies depression that descends for no apparent reason.

Restores serenity, dispels gloom.

- ⊞ for animals that seem "down in spirits" as expressed in lack of vigor and energy, downcast eyes and ears, hanging head, "hang-dog" appearance.

- ⊞ for gloomy **birds**, such as **parrots**, that remove their own feathers.

- ⊞ where owners or handlers feel something is seriously wrong with an animal but don't know what it is.

- ⊞ for illnesses with sudden onset.

## Indications for use:

This remedy is little used in the treatment of animals, because while it may not be apparent, there is usually a reason for an animal's low spirits that needs to be investigated. It may be the loss of a companion, owner, or friend, or simply being with gloomy and depressing people, as in the case of a dog that became depressed every afternoon when the man of the house returned from work and began arguing with his wife. Animals are also sensitive to atmospheres in buildings, and cases where domestic animals have become gloomy following seances in the home have been reported. There are also many accounts in veterinary literature of animals responding to the fate of companions or owners at a distance, so the circumstances promoting the depression may not be evident within an animal's immediate environment.

The problem may reside within the animal rather than its environment. It may be a physical illness, a chemical or hormonal imbalance, or a cancer. In such cases Mustard will not remedy the underlying condition. Tuxworth (1981) provides the following cautionary tale: he prescribed Mustard, together with Wild Rose, for an Irish Setter of normally cheerful disposition that suffered periodically, with apparent resignation, from inexplicable bouts of depression, but to no avail. The attacks became more frequent and the dog began to deteriorate quickly. An autopsy performed at his death shortly afterwards revealed advanced cancer of the spine with a massive tumour in the brain stem itself. The pressure of this mass had caused the gloom, and as Tuxworth observes, "as his 'backbone' had been destroyed, it is no wonder that he lost the will to continue his struggle." **A vet should therefore always be consulted about any animal showing signs of depression apparently unrelated to environmental or circumstantial factors.**

☺ Mustard is nevertheless suitable for depressed animal owners and handlers.

# OAK *(Quercus robur)*

Remedies stoicism and lack of resilience and endurance in normally strong, courageous animals.

Restores resilience, endurance, strength and stamina.

⊞ for animals fighting to survive.

⊞ for normally strong, courageous animals no longer able to struggle against illness or adversity.

⊞ for overworked, exhausted, worn-out animals.

⊞ for animals that don't complain, never give up, ignore natural impulses to rest and keep going despite exhaustion, illness, old age, and infirmity.

⊞ for animals that conceal tiredness or weakness.

⊞ for animals and birds that need occupation and show obsessional behaviors.

⊞ for animals with long illnesses where the animal struggles with one problem after another and keeps winning.

⊞ for sick animals needing strength, especially normally strong animals obviously fighting serious illness, such as cancer, but becoming tired, or struggling to stand and walk despite deterioration of the spine (degenerative myopathy).

## Indications for use:

🐾 All animals that travel great distances to be reunited with their owners.

🐾 **Birds**, such as **parrots**, that spend all day trying to gnaw through a perch or branch. Oak has also proved effective in combination with Olive in treating seabirds poisoned and exhausted by oil slicks and pollution.

🐾 **Cats** that struggle to come through great adversity and suffering, such as a cat that made a full recovery after having been thrown on to a bonfire and severely burned; female cats in constant heat; those that keep going in spite of serious heart disease.

🐾 **Dogs** that will run until they drop, such as **Salukis** and other coursing animals that will pursue their quarry for hours on end; that continue to chase and run despite injuries such as ruptured cruciate ligaments, torn muscles and fractures; house dogs that head for the door when the bell rings despite broken limbs; old dogs who continue to "go through the motions" when their owners persist in taking them to obedience and ringcraft training classes, shows, or other competitions; travellers' dogs and companions of homeless people living in poor conditions and out in all weathers; herding breeds such as the Anatolian that work outdoors in all weathers; pets that will stand in rain and won't seek shelter while watching their owner gardening or working; and sporting and working dogs needing an increase in field stamina.

**Horses** that stand guard while others seek shelter; plod along regardless of age, infirmity, and exhaustion; keep jumping despite bad legs.

**Rodents**, such as **hamsters** and **mice**, that become preoccupied with exercise wheels and continue to use them despite exhaustion.

☺✿ Oak combines well with Olive in cases of illness and exhaustion. It may be helpful to both animals and owners where owners refuse to give up seeking effective treatment for the debilitating or terminal illnesses their animals suffer, exhausting many alternative treatment options.

# OLIVE *(Olea europaea)*

Remedies complete mental and physical exhaustion, fatigue.

Restores strength and the capacity for regeneration.

⊞ for weak, sick, mentally and physically exhausted animals.

⊞ for animals with anemia.

⊞ for animals exhausted from seizures.

⊞ for animals that sleep a good deal after long illness.

⊞ for animals coming out of hibernation.

⊞ for recovery after surgery and convalescence.

⊞ for animals suffering long, stressful conditions such as distemper.

⊞ for animals fragile from birth that cannot cope with strain.

⊞ for revitalization of geriatric animals.

⊞ for animals competing over several successive days.

⊞ for animals lost on the road and self-supporting for any length of time.

## Indications for use:

🐦 **Birds**, especially **seabirds**, suffering exhaustion following storms, gales, extreme weather conditions, oil-slick poisoning and pollution; **racing pigeons** lost or grounded during or after long-distance flights.

🐈 **Cats** lost under floorboards, earthquake rubble, in airplane cargo holds, locked buildings, outbuildings or sheds for days or weeks; exhausted strays; those suffering feline leukemia, or the effects of fights.

🐕 **Dogs** at the end of a long hunting season or in and out for several days in search and rescue operations; competition dogs at the end of long and taxing shows, or after several days competition; those lost for several days. Olive can be given in drinking water before work or competition to prevent tiredness.

🐾 ✿ **Hedgehogs** coming out of hibernation (combine with Water Violet).

🐾 **Horses** before and after hunting, eventing, jumping, racing.

🐾 ✿ **Tortoises** emerging from hibernation (combine with Water Violet).

☺ Olive has been likened to Vitamin C by one vet because of its tonic properties. It is an invaluable standby for animal owners and handlers, not least as an excellent "pick me up" for competitors facing long journeys home after a long day or successive days of competition, hunting or work; for owners, handlers, and vets suffering loss of sleep through attending to sick animals or animals giving birth; for farmers and shepherds during the lambing season; and for owners exhausted looking after companion animals with lingering illnesses such as cancer.

✿ Olive combines well with Hornbeam.

# PINE *(Pinus sylvestris)*

Remedies guilt and contriteness.

Restores positive attitude.

It remains open to question as to whether animals experience feelings of guilt. Many owners believe they do and claim that their animals look guilty when they have stolen food, made a mess, been destructive or aggressive, or in the case of horses, unseated them. Some animals appear to act guiltily by trying to cover up their misdemeanors. More probably, the animal's appearance and behavior express submission and fear because they anticipate punishment for what they have done rather than any sense of guilt. It may therefore be more appropriate to consider their behavior apologetic rather than guilty.

☺ Animals may pick up their owner's feelings of guilt, and Pine is a suitable remedy for people who don't think they have done enough for their pets, blame themselves for not having noticed tell-tale signs of illness, for not having acted quickly enough, for poor decisions and other mistakes.

# RED CHESTNUT *(Aesculus carnea)*

Remedies excessive fear and anxiety for others, and overprotectiveness.

Restores confidence and trust in others and calmness in emergencies.

⊞ for animals overconcerned about their offspring or their owner's children.

⊞ for animals that show exaggerated caring, mother their young too long, or delay weaning them.

⊞ for animals overconcerned about, and overprotective to, their owners.

⊞ for animal mothers that won't let anyone near their young.

⊞ for animal mothers about to be separated from their young, temporarily or permanently.

## Indications for use:

- **Cats** that constantly seek new hiding places for kittens.

- **Cows** that won't let anyone near their calves.

- **Dogs** anxious about their companions or owners; bitches whose puppies are removed for culling, removal of dew claws, veterinary treatment.

- **Horses** anxious for companions after a traumatic event such as a fire.

- ☺ Red Chestnut is normally combined with other remedies for fear and anxiety, notably Aspen and Mimulus. Animals often pick up their owners' overconcern and anxiety and can become neurotic as a result. Red Chestnut is therefore a suitable remedy for anxious, hypochondriacal owners.

# ROCK ROSE *(Helianthemum nummularium)*

Remedies extreme fear and panic, absolute terror.

Restores courage, bravery, and calmness.

- ⊞ for panic and terror when an animal feels cold to the touch, is shaky, and shows signs of extreme fear.

- ⊞ for situations where the animal's terror presents a danger to itself or others.

- ⊞ for agoraphobia, when an animal is terrified to go outside.

- ⊞ for any kind of situation that elicits extreme escape behavior, as when an animal chews, bites, kicks through steel doors, hinges, chain link fences, metal.

- ⊞ in emergency treatment situations when the only alternative is to anesthetize the animal.

- ⊞ for sunstroke, heatstroke with giddiness or unconsciousness.

## Indications for use:

**All animals and birds** that witness terror in others, because terror is contagious in animals. Rock Rose should be administered to the animals experiencing the terror and those that witness it. It can be sprayed on them if they are not reachable or cannot be handled.

**Cats** showing terror with arched back, hair standing on end, hissing, etc. Rock Rose has also been used successfully in treating a cat poisoned through ingestion of an organophosphate insecticide that resulted in alternating mildness and frenzy.

**Horses** that panic easily, putting themselves and others in danger by rearing up and/or falling over. Rock Rose has proved effective for dental work in horses. It is one of the major remedies for use in horses, along with Aspen and Mimulus.

**Poultry** terrorized by a fox, polecat, mink, or other predators.

**Wild animals and birds** can die of terror and so Rock Rose should be administered when they are caught, confined or handled, and in attempts to tame them.

Rock Rose is the specific remedy for terror.

# ROCK WATER

Water from a spring or well, known to have healing power.

Remedies rigidity, tightness and repression.

Restores flexibility, spontaneity, suppleness, and gentleness.

☐ for all kinds of inflexibility – physical, mental and behavioral; physical rigidity and stiffness; training problems; learning difficulties; compulsiveness, such as territorial behavior.

☐ for lack of adaptability and stress associated with changes in routine.

☐ for lack of physical flexibility, suppleness and softness.

☐ for dominant behavior.

+ for hypochondriacal behavior.

+ for self-denying behavior, i.e. nursing mothers that neglect their needs in meeting those of offspring.

+ for stubbornness.

+ for arthritic conditions.

## Indications for use:

🐾 All animals and **birds** that show physical or behavioral inflexibility, learning difficulties, poor ability to cope with changes in routine or status, stubbornness, rigidity, compulsive territorial behavior.

🐾 **Cats**, especially **orientals** and **Persians**, stressed by changes in routine that respond by inconsistent urination, spraying, scratching and biting; that are stressed if their owner returns home later than usual, or by the arrival of visitors; that refuse to eat from anything other than their own bowls; that will only eat certain foods; that will only use a certain litter tray or kind of litter material; **Siamese** and other **orientals** that exhibit hypochondriacal over-reactions (often like their owners) to minor illnesses and ailments – 'giving up the ghost' and refusing to eat.

🐾 **Dogs** that insist on a walk at the same time daily, irrespective of their condition or the weather; that are hard to train or teach new tricks, that don't take commands or listen; that will only eat a certain food or from a certain dish; those who refuse to have a lead put on.

🐾 **Horses** that are more flexible on one side than the other, or that show hypochondriacal behavior, or stubbornness.

☺ It is particularly useful for owners who are hard on themselves and their animals, who adhere to rigid and strict routines and disciplines, and expect animals to perform in specific ways, or to certain standards. One such was John, a forty-five year old businessman, who ran several miles each evening with Sam, his Great Dane/Labrador cross. Sometimes John, with one or other leg bandaged, could be seen pulling the reluctant dog by his lead, and continued to do so, despite warnings from friends and neighbors that his obsessive behavior was potentially harmful to him and his dog. When asked why he pushed himself so hard, John would say that if he did not adhere to such a punishing discipline he felt guilty about eating, which he did to excess each weekend. His behavior was thus an obsessive-compulsive cycle of overindulgence followed by self-denial. John refused to listen to others who urged moderation. He suffered a massive heart attack and died during one of his weekend runs. Sam outlived him by several years, during which he showed disinclination towards exercise of any kind, preferring to stay curled up in front of the fire.

☺ Rock Water is also useful to owners, especially competitors, who push themselves and their animals ruthlessly in order to win; and those who create stress in animals by their strict adherance to disciplines, whether it is 'boot-camp' style training methods or regimes, or lifestyle choices such as exercise and diet. Jack , for instance, was a fanatical vegetarian who fed his boxer dog, Max, largely on a diet of fruit and nuts. Jack refused to accept that this was inappropriate for his canine companion. For his part, the excruciatingly thin but otherwise healthy Max, compulsively begged for or stole food, and frequently escaped to feast on any available garbage, much to his owner's annoyance.

❀ Rock Water may be usefully combined with Rock Rose where an animal shows intense fear, often as a result of having been punished for its stubbornness.

❀ ☺ Rock Rose can also be used with Beech where dominance or aggression is a feature of the animal (or owner's) behavior.

❀ Rock Water combines well with Oak for animals that show compulsive tendencies, such as insisting on going out whatever the weather, or on covering the same distance every time they are exercised, which takes its toll on their strength and stamina.

❀ Similarly, Rock Water can combine with Olive if, as a result of its behavior, the animal is exhausted.

❀ Can be used with Walnut to assist adaptation to life changes.

# SCLERANTHUS *(Scleranthus annuus)*

Remedies uncertainty and imbalance.

Restores stability and balance.

- ⊞ for animals of uncertain temperament, sometimes described as "schizophrenic" by their owners, whose moods fluctuate, and whose behavior alternates between extremes: being outgoing for a time and then withdrawn, friendly one minute and aggressive the next, obedient one day and disobedient the next, over-eating for a time and then refusing all food.

- ⊞ for animals that suffer from sicknesses with unclear, changing symptoms, such as alternating constipation and diarrhea, anorexia and ravenous appetite, temperature fluctuations, symptoms that alternate from better to worse, alternating patterns of recovery and relapse.

- ⊞ for animals that appear confused or disoriented and show erratic "dithery" behavior.

- ⊞ for animals experiencing psychomotor seizures where rebalancing is needed.

- ⊞ for animals with inner ear disorders, loss of balance and/or vertigo.

- ⊞ for travel sickness.

- ⊞ for hormone imbalances.

## Indications for use:

🐾 **Birds**, including free-range **poultry**, whose wings have been clipped, to minimize lopsidedness; and for other wing injuries. Tuxworth (1981) reports the dramatic recovery of a young wild currawong, a crow-like Australian songbird (genus: *Strepera*) also known as the Bell Magpie. It had badly injured the primary flight feathers of its right wing, and in the same accident damaged its left foot so that it hung grotesquely askew. The wing was quite useless for flight as the bird could manage only a few flaps. Confined to an aviary the bird ignored the food offered, and so to avoid unnecessary handling of the bird, Scleranthus was placed in its water supply to help it regain its equilibrium, together with Rescue Remedy (see page 87) for the shock and disorientation it was experiencing. Within a week the claws were strong enough to grip a perch and the bird made a few hesitant hops around the cage. Soon it was fluttering aloft with renewed strength and balance. After a further week both wing and foot were healing well and so the aviary door was left ajar, and the bird flew to freedom in its own time.

**Dogs** of uncertain temperament that, for example, play with a child one moment and then snap at it the next, want to go out one minute and in again the next; that show confusion following the death of an owner; bitches that show changes in temperament and behavior during or following a season, and during false or phantom pregnancies. Scleranthus may also benefit diabetic dogs receiving insulin to help stabilize glucose levels.

**Horses** whose behavior is erratic, doing all that is asked of them one day and refusing the next day.

**Sows** with hormonal imbalance that savage their piglets.

✿ Scleranthus combines well with Walnut in the treatment of animals that appear to be "at death's door" one minute and full of life the next.

☺ It is helpful in dealing with the emotional ups and downs experienced by owners when caring for very sick or terminally ill animals, and may also be useful for owners uncertain about whether or not an aged or ill animal should be given euthanasia.

# STAR OF BETHLEHEM *(Ornithogalum umbellatum)*

Remedies all forms of mental, emotional, or physical shock.

Restores mental, emotional, and physical calmness.

⊞ for shock following accidents, traumatic events, and grief.

⊞ for longstanding trauma such as cruelty and starvation (in such cases it might have to be administered repeatedly for some time).

⊞ for the shock associated with intense emotional or physical pain.

⊞ for birth trauma.

⊞ for numbness resulting from extreme cold.

⊞ for the shock and trauma to bodily tissues triggered by poisoning.

⊞ for allergies and other physical conditions such as diabetes originally triggered by shock or trauma.

⊞ after anesthesia, and post-operatively, as surgery is a shock to the system.

## Indications for use:

🐾 All animals in road traffic accidents, fires, and disaster situations; that are traumatized by gunshot, bombs, etc.; caught in traps and snares. Animal mothers that have lost their offspring at, or soon after, birth.

🐾 **Birds** stunned by flying into windows or cars. Star of Bethlehem was used successfully to treat a cockerel whose comb had been partly bitten off by a fox.

🐾 **Horses** when being broken in, and for those traumatized by training for rodeos, bull fights, etc.

🐾 **Wild animals** and **birds** captured, taken into captivity, handled, or given veterinary treatment.

☺ Star of Bethlehem can be applied to the temples, nose, gums and mouth of unconscious animals to interrupt trauma and trigger immediate healing. It is also recommended for animal owners and handlers subjected to shock or trauma.

# Sweet Chestnut (Castanea sativa)

Remedies extreme mental anguish.

Restores perseverance and endurance despite anguish.

⊞ for animals that have reached the limits of mental or physical endurance and have given up.

+ for animals with a long history of mental or physical suffering resulting from terrible circumstances, cruelty, mistreatment, neglect, or for those whose physical condition appears hopeless following a long debilitating illness.

+ for animals beaten or starved almost to death.

+ for animals that refuse to eat to the point of death after separation from owners.

+ for animals in enforced captivity.

+ for self-mutilation.

+ for animals experiencing difficulty when giving birth.

+ for animals suffering bloat or colic.

+ for animals suffering from severe chronic sickness and severe psychological disturbances.

## Indications for use:

🐾 All animals rescued from terrible circumstances, including vivisection and factory farming.

🐾 **Calves** reared in veal crates or their equivalent (that is, hobbled and kept in total darkness).

🐾 **Cats** tearing themselves apart with ear and/or skin problems.

🐾 **Dogs** tearing themselves apart with ear and/or skin problems; those suffering bloat.

🐾 **Horses** suffering with colic.

🐾 **Ponies** working in mines ("pit ponies"), reaching the end of their tether.

🐾 **Wild animals** suddenly placed in captivity.

✿ Sweet Chestnut is usually administered in combination with other remedies such as Olive which helps endurance. In the treatment of skin conditions it can be applied topically in a spray or lotion.

# VERVAIN *(Verbena officinalis)*

Remedies over-enthusiasm and effort, impulsiveness.

Restores restraint.

- ☐ for intense, enthusiastic, and eager animals that appear "keyed up" or "highly strung" and unable to relax; that overdo things, live on their nerves, and suffer muscle pain.

- ☐ for animals that cannot get enough exercise, are "always on the go", and hyperactive.

- ☐ for exuberant, overwhelming "pushy" animals that knock people over.

- ☐ for hyperactivity.

- ☐ for nervous conditions and complaints.

- ☐ for the management of animals with fractures.

## Indications for use:

🐾 **Cats** that are "highly strung" and tense, keep wandering, and are never still.

🐾 **Dogs** that are too full of energy, on the go all the time, pull and strain on the leash, such as overactive **terriers, Springer Spaniels** and **Border Collies**; and in the management of dogs that need to be restrained and confined to effect full recovery from ruptured cruciate ligaments.

🐾 **Horses** that are like "coiled springs", very tense and unable to relax, or "pushy". They may become rigid with tension because their muscles cannot relax.

✿ Vervain combines well with Chestnut Bud in the treatment of compulsive behaviors.

# V**INE** *(Vitis vinifera)*

Remedies dominance, bullying, territoriality.

Restores positive leadership qualities of natural leaders.

+ for animals that act aggressively to establish dominance over other animals or people and over territory.

+ for animals that appear ruthless in their domination of other animals and people, bullying and frightening them.

## Indications for use:

🐱 All animals that aggressively defend their territory, keeping other animals and owners out of a bed, car, armchair, and won't allow others to come near their food or to take food or toys from them.

🐱 **Cats** showing aggression to other cats and animals, their owners or other humans in defense of themselves or their territory or during play.

Borchelt and Voith (1982, pp.673–681) indicate that:

> *Aggressive behavior in cats is the second most common behavioral complaint of cat owners. The body and facial postures and the context in which aggression occurs provide the information upon which a diagnosis is made. However, it is often difficult to make a definitive diagnosis. Sometimes the aggressive behavior may have started for one reason but continues for another. Sometimes it is not easy to determine the body and facial postures of a cat because they occur too quickly. At other times the cat rapidly alternates between approach, attack, defense and a variety of superimposed postures.*

Therefore, careful observation over time of the behavior of the cat and circumstances in which it occurs may be necessary for accurate diagnosis and choice of remedy.

🌸 May also be useful, in conjunction with Crab Apple, in the treatment of constipation.

🐶 **Dogs** with behavioral problems involving dominance, over-protectiveness, territoriality, and non-acceptance of other animals.

In its annual report (1994) The Association of Pet Behaviour Counsellors identified the two most common presenting problems as aggression towards people and aggression towards other dogs. These are more common in male dogs. Major symptoms of aggression towards people include dominance (for example preventing owners from getting into bed), and territoriality (for example defending a chair, bed or feeding bowl), or overprotectiveness (for example defending the family and home by keeping the postman at bay in the garden; not allowing visitors (human or animal) on to or near the owner's property; not accepting newcomers, such as the owner's new spouse, lover, or baby).

Dominant dogs may come between owners and their friends, quite literally. One owner's courtship was made difficult by his **Saluki**, who would sit between him and his girlfriend, and growl at the slightest indication of contact or intimacy by either of them. He continued to come between them when they married, and never fully accepted the wife.

If forcibly suppressed, a dominant dog may become stressed and more aggressive. These behaviors may be remedied by Vine, but need to be distinguished from fear-based aggression where a dog bites out of fear in selected circumstances, such as when confronted with men with beards, or with people wearing hats or motorcycle helmets, and usually when it cannot make an escape. This kind of aggression may be remedied by Mimulus.

Aggression towards people typically shows an increase in the summer months and at Christmas when dogs generally come into contact with more people during school holidays or when family and friends visit at Christmas. Visits from the postman are also more frequent at Christmas.

Aggression towards other dogs also shows itself in a number of ways – for instance, by struggles over status within the home or kennel, through fear-based aggression and the attacking of other dogs when away from home. Aggression within the home peaks during the winter months when dogs tend to be more confined, whereas aggression away from home, together with fear-based aggression, peaks in the spring months with the increase of dog-walking activities. Dominant and would-be dominant dogs may stand over a subordinate threatening to bite its neck, grab its muzzle, or may slam into its body. Their behavior tends to be confrontative, whereas basically fearful dogs show avoidance behavior and only snap or bite when they cannot avoid confrontation. Vine is suited to the former and Mimulus to the latter.

However, Dr. John Bradshaw of the University of Southampton (1995) points out that while it is fashionable among behaviorists to regard dominance as the cause of most behavioral problems in the dog, it is not necessarily the case that dominant dogs are always aggressive. A dog that is dominant to one person or one dog may be completely submissive to another, dominant under certain circumstances but completely different under others. Dominance or submissiveness depend just as much on the owner as on the dog. Moreover, in a pack of dogs it is quite common for the order of dominance to change and sometimes change back again. This often happens in a litter of puppies where the hierarchy changes more than once as they grow up.

In order to determine the appropriate remedy for the animal showing aggressive behavior, it is necessary to identify the circumstances and stimuli that elicit its aggression.

The following questions should help to identify and isolate the trigger stimulus in any given situation:

*Who or what was threatened by the animal?*

*Where and when did the incident(s) occur?*

*Who or what was present?*

*Where was the animal in relation to the people or other animals in the situation? (For example, was it between the owner and the person being threatened? Did it maintain body contact with the owner when threatening?)*

*What was the owner's response? (Did the owner pet or speak soothingly to the animal in an effort to calm it, and therefore inadvertently reinforce the aggressive behavior?) How do the owners interpret the aggressive behavior? (Does the owner believe the animal is protecting him/her by threatening strangers, protecting itself, or trying to assert itself?)*

A careful and complete history should reveal how the original response was generalized and should enable prediction of formerly unpredictable aggressive behavior through identification of subtle signals previously not recognized by the owner, that may predict an attack. A suitable remedy should then suggest itself. Where dominance underpins aggression, issues of social rank and territory will be identified. In such situations, Vine is indicated as the appropriate remedy, as opposed to Beech where no such issues are involved. Mimulus is indicated for fear-based aggression.

**Caution:** It must be remembered, however, that in some animals aggression may be due to central nervous system disease, tumors, and lesions in the forebrain, or to other serious illness. Owners should therefore consult a vet before treating an aggressive animal with flower essences.

Moreover, even if there is no physical basis for an animal's aggression, treatment with Vine or other flower essences does not guarantee that the animals will never again show aggression, and owners and handlers should be alert to this possibility.

☺ Vine is a suitable remedy for dominant, tyrannical owners and for "macho" owners who encourage similar behaviors in their animals.

# **W**ALNUT *(Juglans regia)*

Remedies difficulties in adapting to new circumstances.

Restores the ability to adapt to change.

- ⊞ for confusion, distress and/or behavioral disorders associated with transitions in life, new surroundings, changes of lifestyle, changes in routine or diet, or changes in the emotional climate of the household.

- ⊞ for females coming into season or heat, especially for the first time.

- ⊞ during pregnancy.

- ⊞ after neutering.

- ⊞ during teething and weaning.

- ⊞ for major lifestyle changes such as when people join or leave the household as in divorce, separation, death of owner or family member, birth of a child.

- ⊞ for animals being re-homed or moving home (or when there are major changes to living environment such as change of furniture or carpets).

⊞  for animals subjected to long journeys or exportation.

⊞  for animals that lose an eye or limb or some physical function such as sight or hearing.

⊞  for the treatment of eruptive skin conditions in animals that develop allergies in response to dietary or environmental change.

⊞  for animals hospitalized for long periods.

⊞  before and after anesthesia.

⊞  prior to euthanasia.

## Indications for use:

🐾 **Birds**, especially males, that incubate for the first time.

🐾 **Cats** during the transition from using an indoor litter tray to outdoor toilet; reaching sexual maturity that begin to spray in the house; elderly cats that become deaf. Elimination problems may also be caused by change in the animal's lifestyle and routine, or in the emotional climate of the home.

🐾 **Dogs** that become aggressive to the remaining owner after the death of a partner; puppies and older dogs when changing homes or owners; geriatric dogs that become blind from glaucoma, cataracts, or other disease or that become deaf.

🐾 **Horses** being broken in, transported for breeding purposes, moved to new environments; changing owners. Walnut has been used successfully (applied to the soft cavity under its foreleg) to break the habit of prancing in a horse.

❀ Walnut combines well with Honeysuckle to break links with the past.

☺ It can be helpful for owners whose animals are about to be given euthanasia to help them adjust to the loss of the animal, and many vets consider it helpful to the animal, easing its transition from life.

# WATER VIOLET *(Hottonia palustris)*

Remedies aloofness, reserve.

Restores social contact.

+ for animals that tend to withdraw from contact with others or their owners, especially when ill, and with whom it is difficult to establish genuine contact.

+ for animals that appear to prefer being on their own or to keep their distance from others.

+ for animals seemingly indifferent to what is going on around them.

+ for the removal of foreign bodies from eyes, ears, skin, etc.

## Indications for use:

🐾 Reserve and aloofness can be characteristic of certain breeds of animal, especially those that instinctively hunt alone or have learned to do so through training. Owners of these independent, self-reliant animals may suspect they have a hearing problem because they don't always respond to approaches or commands. Where the condition is extreme, or occurs in breeds not usually known for their aloofness or reserve, Water Violet may help draw them out.

🐾 **Cats** that are often aloof, especially orientals. Giving Water Violet to cats when they are ill seems to reinforce their inner strength and powers of healing. It is also useful in the handling, socialization, and treatment of feral or semi-feral cats.

🐾 **Dogs**, such as **Afghan Hounds** and **Salukis**, that appear to become deaf to their owners' commands once they give chase, are often wrongly considered unintelligent when they act in accordance with their instincts. Reserve and aloofness are normal characteristics of these breeds and may be regarded as constitutional traits. Water Violet may also be useful for dogs socialized only comparatively late in life; for those that are part wolf, coyote, or dingo, and those, such as **Huskies**, with wild ancestry.

🐾 **Horses** that will not mix with the herd or companion animals and are not friendly to their handlers; **Arabian horses**.

Extreme withdrawal may be a pathological condition, a symptom of illness. It can also result from vaccination against rabies.

However, as Tuxworth (1981) indicates, all animals are instinctive Water Violets in time of sickness. "If we will only be positive Water Violets ourselves and allow them their own space, they will seek solitude, resting and fasting until they heal themselves. At this time of heightened sensitivity we should be as calm and unobtrusive as possible in our desire to help – a few soothing drops in the water supply may be all that is required to tip the scales." Water Violet may also help owners to maintain the appropriate distance from sick animals and give them psychological space in which to heal. Its use is therefore recommended for both animal and owner during an animal's recuperation and convalescence.

✿ It may also assist, in combination with Crab Apple, in the removal of foreign bodies in the eye, ears, skin, etc.

# **W**HITE CHESTNUT *(Aesculus hippocastanum)*

Remedies preoccupation and sleeplessness.

Restores the ability to rest.

⊞ for any obsessive behavior – persistent licking or chewing of the skin or paws until raw, persistent scratching, lashing of the tail.

⊞ for animals restless during sleep.

⊞ for restlessness when giving birth.

⊞ for animals that persistently move their young.

⊞ for illnesses that appear repeatedly such as allergies, rheumatic disorders brought on by the weather.

### **Indications for use:**

🐦 **Birds** restless when egg laying or during incubation.

✿ **Dogs** left alone all day that manifest chronic skin problems through constant licking, scratching or chewing; or that chew furniture and

furnishings. Veterinary dermatologist Richard Harvey (1994) indicates that dogs often begin to scratch because of boredom, and that once this behavior starts it is almost certain to get worse, and sometimes does so very quickly. This can lead to problems such as fly biting, sometimes found in **Cocker Spaniels**; flank biting, common in **Dobermans**; and tail biting, common in **Bull Terriers**; and to related skin diseases. The breeds most likely to suffer from these conditions are unworked working breeds such as **Labradors** and **Dobermans**. In such cases White Chestnut combines well with Impatiens and Wild Oat. In some cases skin disorders follow scratching brought about by a change of diet or environment. Where this is the case White Chestnut should be combined with Walnut.

❀ Stress can also lead to persistent scratching. Where this is a possibility, White Chestnut can be combined with Aspen and Mimulus to treat anxiety and fears underlying the repetitive behavior and restlessness. In all cases of scratching and related skin disorders, White Chestnut should be combined with Crab Apple and with Chestnut Bud to break the bad habit. White Chestnut and Crab Apple are also an appropriate combination where scratching is because of fleas.

# WILD OAT *(Bromus ramosus)*

Remedies lack of direction.

Restores direction of energies and potentials.

⊞ for animals that appear to have great abilities or potentials not coming to fruition.

⊞ for animals that do not perform to their capacities.

⊞ for animals retired from an occupation for which they were bred and trained.

⊞ for animals whose owners vacillate between treating them as working animals or pets.

⊞ for animals prevented from fulfilling natural functions (such as reproduction).

### Indications for use:

🐾All animals trained for, or expected to fulfill, a dual purpose, for example, working and showing.

🐾**Dogs** retired from racing, coursing, working, or showing, and placed in homes as pets; working dogs not worked; dogs in training as guide, hearing, police, or rescue dogs likely to be dropped from, or not accepted for, the program for which they were trained; obedience champions disobedient at home; dogs treated as both pet and guard dogs; **greyhounds** that don't want to race; and bitches with severe false, or phantom, pregnancies.

🐾**Horses** that don't want to race; retired racehorses.

# WILD ROSE (Rosa canina)

Remedies resignation and apathy.

Restores the life force and the will to live.

⊞ for animals in critical conditions when they appear to be giving up and their body is cold.

⊞ for animals during long-term debilitating illness.

⊞ for animals that seem chronically and hopelessly sad, bored, indifferent, and apathetic.

⊞ for animals lacking energy; that do not want to move.

⊞ for total disinterest in food for no apparent reason.

⊞ for animals that appear to be getting no enjoyment from life.

⊞ for abandoned animals in shelter, kennels and for some animals in zoos.

## Indications for use:

- ✿ **Cats** lacking energy and enthusiasm as a result of hypothyroidism may benefit from Wild Rose in combination with Crab Apple.

- ✿ **Horses** that will do nothing for new owners, combine with Honeysuckle.

- 🐑 **Sheep** that frequently get on to their backs and cannot get up.

# Willow *(Salix vitellina)*

Remedies maliciousness and sulkiness.

Restores good temper.

- ⊞ for bad-tempered, sulky animals.

- ⊞ for animals that appear to be acting out of spite by excessive or inappropriate urination, such as on the owner's bed, and destructiveness, especially of the owner's property.

## Indications for use:

- 🐱 Animals that appear to be acting out of spite. Such animals are really only reacting to challenges to their territory or status from humans or other animals by marking their territory. Urination and destructiveness are reactions to stress and may also occur in animals that have been abused or have been overtrained zealously or with physical violence.

- 🐱 **Cats** not using the litter box. Borchelt and Voith (1982, p.673) indicate that "the most common behavior problem reported by cat owners is elimination out of the litter box. This problem can be due to disease, territoriality, stress, or learning difficulties. It may also be because the owner does not recognize that cats may object to litter trays smelling of daisies and other deodorizers and much prefer the smells the owner is trying to obliterate." Nevertheless, many owners attribute it to

spitefulness. They may punish the cat, thereby increasing the cat's anxiety and reinforcing the problem, or may begin to resent it, in which case they should take Willow themselves.

**Horses** refusing to take the bit.

☺ Willow may be useful for vets who resent the demands made upon them by clients or colleagues.

# EMERGENCY REMEDIES/ESSENCES

Emergency remedies are prepared remedies that combine several flower essences for use in emergency situations. These include Healing Herbs Five Flower Remedy, Ellon USA's Calming Essence, the Rescue Remedy developed by Dr. Edward Bach, the Kennel Remedy, developed by a US veterinarian for use on any occasion when an animal is left at home by itself or put into kennels (this combines Walnut, Honeysuckle, Chicory, Scleranthus, and White Chestnut with the Bach Rescue Remedy), and Aubrey Westlake's Radiation Remedy (a combination of Cherry Plum, Star of Bethlehem, Rock Rose, Gentian, Vine, Walnut and Wild Oat). Crystal Herbs' Emergency Essence and Sun Essences' Emergency Essence also conform to the same formula as the Rescue Remedy.

The combination of flower essences produced and distributed under the trade name Rescue Remedy is widely considered to be the single most important remedy in healing animals. It has been described (Case 1989) as "a first-aid kit in a bottle". Often it is all that is needed to "rescue" them from their predicament and restore normal functioning. It is an invaluable quick-acting remedy for use in emergencies and has undoubtedly saved the lives of many animals (see Vlamis 1994). Many vets use it routinely to calm animals and birds before examining them, before and after surgery and many other treatments. It is often the first line of approach because shock is a major factor in many conditions affecting animals, and because as many as 90% of animal problems are fear related and can be helped by relaxation. Rescue Remedy does not interfere with the other flower essences, but works synergistically to reinforce their effects.

**Rescue Remedy** or equivalent composite combine:

**Impatiens** *(Impatiens glandulifera)* to deal with the impatience, irritability, and agitation often accompanying stress that sometimes result in muscle tension and pain;

**Clematis** *(Clematis vitalba)* the remedy for unconsciousness, "spaciness" and faintness that often accompany trauma;

**Rock Rose** *(Helianthemum nummularium)* the remedy for terror, panic, hysteria, and great fear;

**Cherry Plum** *(Prunus cerasifera)* the remedy for loss of mental or physical control;

**Star of Bethlehem** *(Ornithogalum umbellatum)* the remedy for mental and physical trauma.

It remedies stress, distress, and tension, and restores calm, reassurance, relaxation.

It may be used:

- ☐ as an adjunct to any other treatment used for and during immediate crisis resulting from accident, dental treatment, injury, shock, surgery, trauma.

- ☐ as a safe alternative to sedatives and tranquilizers.

- ☐ as an adjunct to light anesthesia for small animals such as **chinchillas**, **rabbits**, **squirrels**, etc.

- ☐ to combat the depressing effects of anesthesia in animals born under caesarean section, and to revive them.

- ☐ in anesthetic crisis when heart and breathing stops, and during cardiac arrest.

- ☐ to resuscitate animals whose breathing has stopped, or where there is acute respiratory difficulty.

- ☐ in cases of choking caused by spasm of the larynx.

- ☐ after convulsions.

- ☐ to revive weak animals after birth.

- ☐ to revive animals slow to recover from anesthesia.

⊞ to speed recovery in cases of heatstroke and exhaustion.

⊞ to help wounds heal more quickly.

⊞ to treat a wide variety of conditions, including bites (insect and animal), burns, colic, convulsions, heatstroke, injuries, nervousness, paralysis, poisoning, snakebite, sneezing, sudden collapse, torsion, wounds.

## Indications for use:

🐾 All animals and **birds** visiting vets. It helps to relieve tension, which may mask the true nature of the presenting problem, makes for easier examination, and presents a truer picture of the animal's condition and normal reactions than if the animal is tense. (Apply 2 drops directly to the tongue).

🐾 Animals being groomed by their owners relax more easily when Rescue Remedy is given, and it is recommended for use prior to any visit to the grooming parlor. Groomers report fewer bites and scratches when Rescue Remedy is given to their charges.

🐾 Animal handlers and drivers report that Rescue Remedy given in drinking water helps them to deliver animals in good condition, and pet shop owners selling small animals and birds can benefit by administering Rescue Remedy in drinking water. Animals caged in pet shops or in animal hospitals, veterinary clinics, etc., can benefit from Rescue Remedy or an equivalent emergency essence sprayed into the environment by way of an atomizer. This will relax the animals and enhance their general well-being.

🐾 All animals involved in road traffic accidents or other accidents where animals are shocked and/or injured. Those suffering from diabetes where stress increases the need for insulin.

🐾 Rescued animals under stress. For those remaining in shelters and rescue accommodation for long periods Rescue Remedy can be added to the drinking water.

🐾 Animals in training learn better when relaxed.

🐾 **Bees** that suffer distress at human hands by apiarists who water down the bees' honey to increase profits, leaving the bees weak and prone to disease that can spread throughout the hive, or who kill the queen and replace her with a more docile one in order to facilitate the robbing of the hive.

🐾 **Birds** should always be given Rescue Remedy no matter what condition they are suffering from, as they are easily stressed and go into shock very quickly. It has been used successfully in the treatment of birds ranging from 19-gram finches to 1356-gram ravens. Rescue Remedy or its equivalent, should be given to all birds before receiving treatment or procedures such as wing wrapping, leg splinting, wound debriding, or when banding for release. Where possible they should be placed in the dark for a short while after its administration. It can be given to birds attacked by cats, blown ashore during severe storms, stunned by flying into windows and cars and to fledglings that have fallen from the nest. One vet reports that a dove that had been hit by a car and suffered a dented skull could be released three days after Rescue Remedy was administered. Rescue Remedy has also been used successfully to relax egg-bound birds and chickens enabling them to lay their eggs. To administer, apply 1 drop at a time to the tip of the lower mandible. The beak should be held open, if possible, to prevent the bird breaking the glass dropper or contaminating it. Otherwise, a drop should be applied to the tip of the beak.

🐾 **Butterflies** that are weak upon emerging from their cocoons.

🐾 **Cats** attacked by other cats or dogs; fading kittens; cats suffering from diabetes, kidney or bladder stones.

🐾 **Chipmunks, squirrels, other rodents**, and small animals mauled by cats or trodden on by horses.

🐾 **Dogs** in car accidents; fading puppies; tiny newborn puppies in breeds such as **Yorkshire Terriers** and **Chihuahuas**. It has been used successfully in the treatment of torsion in an **Irish Wolfhound**.

🐾 **Fish** taken from their natural environment; suffering shock from change in water temperature or PH factor; exposed to glaring bright lights, jolts, or tapping on the aquarium, to human intervention during cleaning and water changes; or that seem lethargic or ill. (1 drop to 10 gallons of water).

🐾 **Horses** when traveling, being shipped or air freighted any distance (administer in their drinking water); when visiting the farrier or being clipped, during show grooming, and similar activities; to prevent race horses and competition animals becoming sweated and nervous; to stimulate healthy feet in those that have become weak and brittle (apply daily in cream form, see p.91); and in cases of colic. Rescue Remedy reduces the pain and distress of colic and has been reported as occasionally eliminating all colic symptoms completely. (Give every few minutes, by mouth if possible). Rescue Remedy may also be used as a precautionary measure to minimize stress reactions that may trigger colic. Changes in weather are thought to trigger colic in some horses. Where this is suspected, giving a dose of Rescue Remedy any time there is a major change in air pressure or temperature may eliminate the problem. Given 12 to 20 minutes after mating, it can reduce stress reactions leading to heart attacks in stallions, which is a major cause of death. It can also be given to mares after mating, during labor and after delivery to reduce stress, and it will stimulate the life force if given to newly born foals.

- Rescue Remedy can be given in any situation where a **horse** is nervous, resistant, panicky, or apprehensive in any way, as an alternative to tranquilizers. It has no known side effects and no recovery period so there is no delay before the horse can be used again.

- **Insects** of all kinds. (1 drop in dilution)

- **Lambs**, especially hill lambs, suffering the effects of difficult births, bruising, shock, exhaustion, and exposure; and from colic.

- **Rabbits** mauled by cats and dogs.

Rescue Remedy is prepared in liquid form and as a cream (Rescue Remedy Cream). The liquid is given orally. Four drops in water is the recommended dose, but if no liquid is available, it may be dropped directly on to the tongue. It should be remembered, however, that animals generally dislike the taste of alcohol, and that the remedy is therefore more acceptable and more easily administered when given in liquid. During recovery from shock or stress Rescue Remedy can be added to drinking water, milk, or other fluids.

Rescue Remedy can also be applied externally when an animal is unconscious by being rubbed into the gums, lips, nostrils or skin, pulse points or soft cavities; and can be dripped onto bandages and gauze directly covering wounds. Rescue Remedy Cream can be applied to bruises, contusions, saddle sores, wounds, etc.

In emergencies dosage will vary depending on the severity of the condition to be treated. The following guidelines have been provided by vets who have used emergencies remedies successfully in treatment:

- bladder stones: 3 drops every 2–4 hours until stones have been passed.

- bleeding: give 2 drops by mouth if the animal is weak or restless.

- if breathing has stopped rub 2 drops into the gums every 5 minutes until breathing is restored. For **birds** apply 1 drop to the tip of a beak every 5 minutes.

- burns: 2 drops on the tongue every 30 minutes.

- choking: 2 drops rubbed into gums will relax the larynx.

- colic: 2 drops every 15 minutes.

- diabetes: 3 drops twice daily.

- gunshot wounds: 2 drops every 5 minutes.

- fractures: 2 drops orally every 30 minutes.

- heart failure: if the heart has stopped beating rub 2 drops into the gums every 5 minutes until heartbeat is restored.

- heatstroke: 2 drops every 10 minutes and transport animal to veterinary clinic immediately.

- nervousness: 2 drops every five minutes.

- nosebleed: 2 drops in mouth every 15 minutes.

- pancreatitis: 2 drops 4 times daily.

- paralysis: 2 drops every 5 minutes.

- poisoning: 2 drops every 5 minutes until veterinary attention is provided.

- rattlesnake strike: 2 drops by mouth every 5–10 minutes.

- snakebite: 2 drops by mouth every 5–10 minutes.

- severe itching: 2 drops every 15 minutes.

- sneezing: 2 drops by mouth every 15 minutes.

- sudden collapse: 2 drops rubbed into gums every 5 minutes.

- wounds: 2 drops every 5 minutes.

> **Caution:** Rescue Remedy is *NOT* a replacement for veterinary care; nor does it work indefinitely. While it helps an animal get over initial shock, further treatment may be needed and should be obtained as quickly as possible.

Rescue Remedy can be used by vets, owners, and handlers for shock when they are involved in accidents or have received injuries from bites or kicks, and to calm themselves during emergencies. It is also useful for owners shocked to discover their animal has a terminal condition.

Calming Essence, Ellon USA's brand of this formula, is also produced in liquid and cream form. In liquid form it can be used for any situation that is stressing or traumatizing an animal, and can be used to stabilize all large and small birds, animals, and fish, regardless of breed, before, during, and after any trauma. It can be given as often as is necessary to assist an animal in calming down when nervous, irritable, panicky, before, during, and after surgery or accident. It can be used to reduce stress, producing a non-sedative calming effect in animals that react adversely to strangers in the home, visits to the vet's clinic, domestic arguments or upheaval, thunder and lightening, and separation from owners or other animals. It is also indicated for weak or injured animals, difficult births, newly born animals; during recovery from surgery and anesthesia; for over-exposure to severe weather; for stress associated with illness or injury; for animals suffering competition stress; and for colic. It should be administered every three to five minutes until improvement is shown.

Calming Essence Cream can be applied topically to help reduce pain, swelling, and inflammation of insect bites, burns, bruises, bumps, and sprains, and to accelerate the healing process. (Case 1994, p.11)

The Emergency Essence and Emergency Essence Cream offered by Healing Herbs are applicable to the same conditions as those above, and in the same ways.

## FLOWER ESSENCE SUMMARY CHART

| Essence | Remedies | Restores | Keynote |
|---|---|---|---|
| Agrimony | concealed distress | inner peace | subtle signs of distress: panting, rapid heart rate |
| Aspen | fear of unknown things | courage | apprehension |
| Beech | intolerance | tolerance, flexibility | bad temper |
| Centaury | lack of assertiveness | assertiveness, resistance | submissiveness, compliance |
| Cerato | lack of confidence | confidence | approval seeking, overall *lack of confidence* |
| Cherry Plum | uncontrollable behavior, compulsiveness | control | *extreme fear, recurring phobias* |
| Chestnut Bud | failure to learn from experience | ability to learn | learning difficulties, repetitive behavior |
| Chicory | possessiveness, attention seeking | normal caring and protectiveness | possessiveness |
| Clematis | absentmindedness | alertness | absentmindedness |
| Crab Apple | uncleanliness, infection, poisoning | cleanliness, dignity | any condition needing cleansing |
| Elm | inadequacy | competence | being overwhelmed |

| Essence | Remedies | Restores | Keynote |
|---------|----------|----------|---------|
| Gentian | discouragement | perseverance | setback |
| Gorse | hopelessness | endurance | despair |
| Heather | loneliness | quiet composure | noisiness, inattentiveness |
| Holly | malice | harmlessness | intense dislike |
| Honeysuckle | homesickness | adjustment to present circumstances | inability to cope with *present* circumstances |
| Hornbeam | weakness | vitality | unresponsiveness |
| Impatiens | impatience | patience | irritability |
| Larch | hesitancy, loss of confidence | confidence | *loss of confidence* |
| Mimulus | fear of known things | courage | nervousness |
| Mustard | depression | serenity | gloominess |
| Oak | lack of resilience in normally strong animals | resilience | persistence in spite of adversity |
| Olive | mental and physical exhaustion | strength | fatigue and exhaustion |
| Pine | guilt, contriteness | positive attitude | apologetic behavior |
| Red Chestnut | overprotectiveness | confidence, trust | *overconcern* |
| Rock Rose | terror | courage, calm | terror, hysteria |

| Essence | Remedies | Restores | Keynote |
|---|---|---|---|
| Rock Water* | rigidity, tightness, repression | flexibility, spontaneity, suppleness, and gentleness | Inflexibility |
| Scleranthus | imbalance, uncertainty | stability, balance | imbalance, fluctuating features |
| Star of Bethlehem | mental, emotional, and physical shock | mental, emotional, and physical calm | shock, trauma |
| Sweet Chestnut | extreme mental and physical distress | endurance | intense pain and distress |
| Vervain | overenthusiasm, impulsiveness | restraint | hyperactivity |
| Vine | dominance, territoriality | positive leadership qualities | aggression involving status and territory |
| Walnut | difficulty adapting to new circumstances | adaptability | coping with change |
| Water Violet | aloofness, reserve | social contact | indifference |
| White Chestnut | preoccupation, sleeplessness | ability to rest | restlessness |
| Wild Oat | lack of direction | direction | unfulfilled potential |
| Wild Rose | resignation | the will to live | apathy |
| Willow | maliciousness | good temper | spitefulness |

*not a flower essence

# PART III

# Directions for Use

# How to Choose the Correct Remedy or Remedy Combination

Flower remedies/essences treat the emotional disorder or dis-ease underlying an animal's behavioral or physical symptoms, that is, the cause and not the effect. This may or may not be apparent to the owner or vet. Selection of the appropriate essence or essences therefore relies on careful systematic observation of the animal's behavior and the circumstances in which it occurs. Broadly speaking, flower essences can be used to remedy constitution, or type, and mood.

## CONSTITUTIONAL OR TYPE REMEDIES

Constitutional remedies treat the fundamental character traits, temperament, and behavior of an animal; these are inborn or innate **constitutional** features and are often, although not necessarily, typical of a particular species or breed of animal. Jupp (1990) suggests that Agrimony fits many **Irish Wolfhounds** because as a breed they are stoical about suffering and manage to appear cheerful and wag their tails even when in a bad way, whereas Water Violet may be suited to more reserved and independent species, such as cats, or breeds such as the **Saluki** or the **Arabian horse**. Oak seems particularly suited to hardy species and breeds, such as flock-guarding breeds of dogs, and ponies, such as the **Shetland**, **Exmoor**, or **Connemara**. However, as Jupp points out, flower essences should be chosen to suit the individual animal, and it is therefore inappropriate to generalize too much about breed type.

## MOOD REMEDIES

Flower essences can also be used to remedy more transient mood states. These *mood* remedies can be used regardless of an animal's constitutional type, and as several flower essences can be given at the same time, both constitutional and mood remedies can be combined in any treatment.

## CHOOSING AN ESSENCE OR ESSENCE COMBINATION

**STEP ONE:** When using flower essences in the treatment of animals, it is necessary to carefully observe and take note of the animal's constitutional, or character, type; its mood; presenting problem; behavioral signs and symptoms; the situation(s) in which they occur; and the nature of the relationship between the animal, and its owners or handlers, with a view to establishing the source of its dis-ease. This may be quite clear-cut or may be revealed only gradually through close examination of the whole pattern of the animal's life involving a detailed behavior inventory (guidance on how to compile a behavior inventory is given below).

Where the animal's problem is clear-cut and you are fairly certain about the **underlying** condition, you may find it helpful to consult the summary chart on page 94. This gives a very **general** overview of the **underlying condition** remedied by each essence, the essence's principal effects, and the keynote, or most characteristic indication, for its use. *It does not detail the many behavioral or physical disorders symptomatic of this condition*. It may help you to choose the correct essence or essence combination for a particular condition. For example, if the animal is frightened of thunderstorms, Mimulus, the remedy for fear of known things, is appropriate, rather than Aspen, which remedies unknown fears.

**STEP TWO:** Having identified the most appropriate essence, you should then refer to it in the directory. This will provide you with a profile of the essence, details of the underlying condition remedied by this essence, behavioral and physical disorders symptomatic of this condition, indications for its use, and other essences with which it can be combined. If these details match your animal's condition, then you can feel confident that it is the appropriate remedy. If the details given do not match the presenting problem of the animal in question, or if, having read the indications for use, you are still unsure of the appropriateness of a particular essence, you should refer to the principal signs and symptoms in the index at the back of the book. The entries under each will refer you to appropriate essences in the directory. The most commonly cited essence is likely to be the most appropriate, and you should consult this first, before referring to the other essences indicated.

Many conditions are not as clear-cut as fear of thunderstorms. If you are unaware of, or uncertain about, the condition underlying the animal's problem, *but fairly clear about what the signs and symptoms are*, you should refer to these in the index at the back of the book, commencing with the principal signs and symptoms and progressing to more minor ones. The entries under each should refer you to the appropriate essences in the directory. The most commonly referred to essence is likely to be the most appropriate remedy, but it may be that no one essence will remedy the condition and that a combination of essences is required. Details of suitable combinations for use in the treatment of specific conditions is listed under each entry in the directory.

If having consulted the chart, index, and directory you are still unclear about the appropriate essence(s), *or if you are uncertain about the signs and symptoms to look up in the index*, you should return to **Step One** and take a very careful inventory of the animal's behavior, circumstances, and relationships. Details of how to do so follow.

When you have identified relevant signs and symptoms, refer to these in the index, commencing with the **major** ones and progressing through to minor ones. The entries under each will direct you to appropriate essences listed in the directory. You should consult each of these and identify the one(s) that fit most closely the overall pattern of signs and symptoms presented by the animal. The closer the match the more confident you can feel that you have chosen the correct remedy. If you cannot choose between two apparently similar essences, or if the symptoms to be treated seem to require more than one essence, these should be combined. You will note that various essence combinations are recommended for certain conditions.

## HOW TO TAKE A BEHAVIOR INVENTORY

Animals have several basic needs in life: survival (fighting and overcoming, or fleeing from anything threatening to hurt or kill them); eating and drinking; housing and hygiene; reproducing; and socializing. If these basic needs are not met problems arise. Whyte (1989) indicates that the gap between what the animal needs and what it gets is often filled by "crime", or undesirable behavior, and when the "crime gap" is closed up, undesirable behavior becomes minimal. The gap between the animal's needs and what it gets may also be filled by physical illness. The signs and symptoms of these diseases and disorders may therefore provide clues to the underlying problem or need state. You may be able to identify this by answering the following questions:

*Does the animal appear content?*

*If not, what are the signs and symptoms of its dis-ease?*

*Is it eating and digesting its food normally?*

*Is it drinking normally?*

*Are its skin, hair, fur, or feathers healthy and clean?*

*Are its elimination behaviors (urination and defecation) normal?*

*Is it sleeping and resting normally?*

*How does it relate to other animals and humans?*

*Does it have any fears?*

*Does it have any bad habits?*

*How would you describe its energy level?*

*How would you describe its mood?*

*Does it appear tense or relaxed?*

*Does it move stiffly or freely?*

*Is it noisy?*

*Does its body feel cold or hot?*

## ARE YOU A FACTOR IN THE ANIMAL'S PROBLEM?

Animals are often obliged to try and fulfill various needs through their owners. Moreover, owners also attempt to fulfill certain needs through animals, and it is often important to identify both sets of needs.

People often fail to recognize stress in animals because they have come to regard the conditions they impose on them as normal. We may think it normal for a horse to be confined in a 12-foot-by-12-foot stall, for birds to be caged, or for a dog to be chained, and for these animals to socialize only with humans on human terms. In most cases, we have removed from animals their natural territory, pack, pack leader, working and hunting opportunities and substituted a quite unnatural domestic situation. Behaviors such as biting, bucking, chewing, smelling, scratching, kicking, rearing, which occur quite normally in the animal's natural environment, may be considered problems when they are in this environment. It is therefore important to recognize that physical and behavioral disorders in animals may have their origins in how the animal has been treated by humans, including yourself.

The most common mistake most owners make is thinking that animals are human, and attributing to them human characteristics, personality traits, and emotions. When this happens the owner does not see the animal as it really is but as a projection of his or her own characteristics. This can lead to a distortion in the relationship between the animal and its owner and to misinterpretation of its behavior.

The nature of the animal–owner relationship is often determined by the way the owner views the animal, that is, whether it is perceived as a child substitute, a status symbol, a means of gaining prestige, a compensation for other relationships that are lacking, a functional tool, work companion, or best friend. Tendencies to mythologize, idealize or romanticize animals in these roles tends to obscure the real nature of their problems.

### To Find Out if You are Part of the Animal's Problem, answer the following questions:

*Why did you choose to own or handle this kind of animal, and this animal in particular?*

*Is the animal like you in its behavior and reactions?*

*In what ways is the animal similar to you?*

*Are the animal's problems similar to those you have or have had in the past?*

*Do you and the animal suffer from similar diseases?*

*Did you ever worry that the animal might get the problem from which it is now suffering?*

*What thoughts typically go through your mind when the animal appears ill or behaves in ways that concern you?*

*How do you typically react when the animal appears ill or behaves in ways that concern you?*

*Does the animal seem particularly upset or disturbed by certain circumstances, changes, tensions, atmospheres, or conflicts in its environment?*

*What messages might you be communicating to it quite unintentionally and unconsciously?*

*What was happening before the animal first showed signs of the illness or behavioral problem?*

*Does the animal get any special attention or different treatment when it starts to show these signs and symptoms?*

*Do you enjoy taking care of a sick animal?*

*Do you ever upset the animal? If so, how?*

*Do you or anyone else ever take out your tensions, anxieties, stresses, upsets, resentments on the animal?*

*Do you or any other person try to control and dominate the animal?*

*Do you allow it to control and dominate you?*

*How often is your social and/or working life disrupted by the animal?*

*Are you very anxious about your animal's welfare and well-being?*

(Source: Pitcairn, 1989)

If, having completed the inventory, you feel that you may be a significant factor in your animal's problems, refer to your major personality, emotional, or behavioral characteristics in the index or to the signs and symptoms of your most common ailments. The remedies that are suited to you are most likely to work for your animals. Indeed, Leslie Kaslof (1991) indicates, "Most animal personality traits, behavioral patterns, and emotional reactions, bear striking resemblance to those same patterns in humans. After studying the indications for Bach Remedy use, put yourself in the animal's place, feel what he feels, sense what he senses, then determine which of the indications most closely fit your animal's behavior patterns, personality traits, and/or emotions."

# Administration & Dosage

**STORAGE OF FLOWER ESSENCES**

Flower essences are supplied in stock bottles in concentrated form and will keep indefinitely if stored correctly. They should be stored away from strong electro-magnetic fields emanating from television sets, microwave ovens, and other electrical appliances. Exposure to direct sunlight and high temperatures should also be avoided. The vial or bottle should always be closed tightly between treatments.

**DIRECTIONS FOR USE**

Each stock bottle of concentrate will make approximately 45 treatment bottles. To prepare a treatment bottle 2 drops of the chosen essence or essences (normally not more than five essences on average in any one treatment) should be added to a 30 ml (1 fluid ounce) bottle of natural spring water, bottles of which can be obtained from most supermarkets and health food stores. Where Rescue Remedy or equivalent is used, 4 drops should be added to the treatment bottle. If only tap water is available this should preferably be boiled before use.

A prepared treatment bottle will remain fresh for some three weeks if stored in a cool place. Otherwise a spoonful of brandy or cider vinegar may be used to preserve it.

**DOSAGE**

Flower essences are administered in drops, a single drop at a time. They are normally given by mouth. Five days is the average period of treatment, although they can be continued for two weeks or longer.

Dosage varies with the particular situation and the animal species being treated. The standard dose is 4 drops. More drops are not harmful, but wasteful. Fewer drops can be used if the animal is quite small (**chipmunks,**

**gerbils**, **guinea pigs**, **hamsters**, **mice**, newly born animals, **rabbits**, **squirrels**, etc). For large breeds of dog and for **sheep** and **goats**, 6 drops should be administered and 10–15 drops for larger animals such as **cows** and **horses**.

These should be given from the treatment bottle as often as needed but at least four times daily. If the condition being treated is very serious administer the essences as needed.

## APPLICATION

In emergency situations, apply before veterinary attention and as an adjunct to veterinary treatment.

If the patient has serious symptoms or you are unsure about the nature of the symptoms, consult a vet as soon as possible.

**DIRECTLY BY MOUTH:** The drops can be applied directly onto or under the animal's tongue, dropped onto the animal's nose where they can be licked off, rubbed into the gums and lips, or into the nostrils of large animals; and dropped onto the tip of birds' beaks, as capillary action will draw the liquid inside the mouth. This method of application is preferable for injured animals and birds, first aid treatment, and in all cases of emergency.

**IN DRINKING WATER, OTHER FLUIDS, AND FOOD:** The drops can be administered in drinking water, milk, or other fluids, with food, on sugar lumps or other treats and given once or twice daily, preferably at the same time each day.

For large dogs, or giants such as **Irish Wolfhounds**, **Great Danes**, and **St. Bernards**; and for sheep or goats, 6 drops should be added to a gallon of water.

For larger animals such as **cows**, **horses**, etc., 10–15 drops should be added to a gallon of water.

However, applying essences in drinking water or food is not very reliable as one cannot easily be sure how much, if any, has been taken. The method works well for animals that drink regularly from their own waterer, or eat regularly. It is recommended for wild animals or those that react badly to being handled and for animals being treated for non-emergency conditions.

**SPRAYS:** Several drops of flower essence(s) can be mixed and sprayed onto the body and into the air surrounding an animal or bird. This method works well with frightened animals and birds that cannot be handled, and with aquatic and marine animals and fish. Spraying onto the animal's nose or mouth may provoke licking. Care should be taken, however, as some animals may react strongly to being sprayed.

**Lotions** comprising a few drops of indicated remedies can be applied topically where pain, stiffness, or inflammation is present. These can be applied to pulse points, to the soft cavities of the body such as under the leg or arm, rubbed into the skin, or when diluted, sprayed onto skin and fur.

**Baths and washes:** Bathing or sponging the animal with water to which a few drops of flower essence(s) has been added may also be useful.

## Effects of Treatment

Animals respond with great immediacy to correctly selected essences. The effects may be immediate or overnight but may take much longer.

If there is a good response the dose should be gradually decreased until there is no further improvement. If there is a relapse the treatment may need to be administered for another period of five days.

If there is no apparent change in the animal's condition, continue to administer the essence for five days. If after five days there is no response, it is probably the wrong remedy. Should this occur, or where more than five remedies appear to be indicated, administer one of the following:

> **Star of Bethlehem**, *where confusion can be traced to shock and trauma of whatever duration;*
>
> **Wild Oat**, *where anxiety or withdrawal are predominant; or*
>
> **Holly,** *where the animal to be treated is of an active or intense disposition.*

Continue to administer this essence on its own until balance is attained or there is a clearer indication of the further essences required.

**Side effects:** Flower essences are safe to take alone, in combination with each other and with other medications, including allopathic drugs and homeopathic remedies. They are harmless, and overdose is impossible. They are sold in the USA as over-the-counter remedies and are available as such in the USA and UK without prescription. There are no known serious side effects, and if the incorrect essence is administered it will simply have no effect. The essences are preserved in alcohol, however, and animals generally dislike the taste. Where possible the essences should be given in water or other fluids as directed previously.

Flower essences can be safely combined with other treatments and will not interfere with their effects. Indeed they may act as important catalysts for healing when used in conjunction with other treatments, especially homeopathy. Richardson-Boedler (1994) indicates that deep-reaching, accelerated healing effects can be observed when Bach Flower Remedies and homeopathic remedies are combined.

Flower essences may also work to good effect when conventional treatments do not. Brennan (1994) observes that when an animal is not responding to conventional treatment, it is advisable to try flower remedies to determine whether the source of the problem may be emotional. She observes that one dose may dramatically improve the animal's physical condition by first acting on the underlying mental state.

# APPENDIX

## Resource guide – sources of remedies discussed in this book

Bach Flower Remedies and other flower essences are widely available as over-the-counter preparations in many pharmacies and health food stores. While not an exhaustive listing, many can also be obtained from the following:

### IN THE UK

**The Bach Centre, Mount Vernon, Bakers Lane, Sotwell, Oxon, England OX10 0PZ**
Tel: 01491 834678          Fax: 01491 825022          http://www.bachcentre.com
Supplies remedies, books and details of courses.

**Celestial Remedies, Doreen Paige, Natural Line Distribution Centre, Unit 12, Belfont Estate, Mucklow Hill, Halesowen, West Midlands, England B62 8DR**
Tel: 0121 585 0025          Fax: 0121 585 0226.
Supplies remedies for animal treatment by mail order, and by way of trade stands at major championship dogs shows in the UK.

**Crystal Herbs, Waveney Lodge, Hoxne, Suffolk, England IP21 4AS**
Tel/Fax: 01379 668848     http://www.goldenage-reiki.com/
Offers the traditional English Remedies as well as a range of flower, gem, crystal essences, courses, tapes and publications.

**Findhorn Flower Essences, Wellspring, 31 The Park, Findhorn, Forres, Moray, Scotland IV36 0TY**          http://www.findhorn.org/business/floweressences/index.html
Tel: 01309 690129          Fax: 01309 691300     e-mail: floweressence@findhorn.org
Supplies products, publications, workshops and consultations.

**Healing Herbs, Julian & Martine Barnard, P.O. Box 65, Hereford, England HR2 0UW**          http://dialspace.dial.pipex.com/town/estate/pc58/
Tel: 01873 890218          Fax: 01873 890314          e-mail: pc58@dial.pipex.com
and from Flower Essence Services, P.O. Box 1769, Nevada City, CA 95959, USA.
Authentic source for the flower remedies of Dr. Bach, tapes, books, posters and courses.

**International Flower Essence Repertoire, The Living Tree, Milland, Nr. Liphook, Hants. England GU30 7JS**
Tel: 01428 741572          Fax: 01428 741679          e-mail: flower@atlas.co.uk
Distributes flower essences from around the world, books and details of workshops.

**Neal's Yard Remedies, Mail Order: Unit 1, St. James House, St. James Square, Manchester, England N2 6DS**
Tel/fax: 0161 831 7875

**Sun Essences, P.O. Box 728, Norwich, England NR3 1UT**
Tel: 0700 785337        http://www.sun-essences.co.uk/
e-mail: sunessences@aol.com
Offers the Sun Essences Traditional Collection, preparation based on Dr. Bach's instructions, Emergency Essence and individual Solarblends, Remedies for people and pets, as well as consultations, lectures, posters and prints.

## IN THE US:

**Flower Essence Services, P.O. Box 1769 Nevada City, CA 95959**
Tel: 1 800 548 0075/1 530 265 0258        Fax: 1 530 265 64 67
http://www.floweressence.com        e-mail info@floweressence.com
US source for Healing Herbs Ltd (UK), as well as the FES Quintessentials North American Flower Essences, books and seminars.

**Global Health Alternatives, 193 Middle Street, Portland, ME 04101**
Tel: 1 800 547 1295/1 207 772 7234        e-mail: info@healthalt.com
http://www.wowpages.com/gha/ellon.html
Formerly Ellon USA, source of Ellon Traditional Flower Remedies, Ellon's Calming Essence.

**Flower Vision Research, P.O. Box 43628 Upper Montclair, NJ 07043**
Tel: 1 800 298 4434/1 973 746 5798        Fax:1 973 746 4321
http://www.flowervr.com        e-mail: essences@flowervr.com
Distributes flower essences from around the world, books and details of workshops.

**NelsonBach USA, Wilmington Technology Park, 100 Research Drive, Wilmington, MA 01887-4406**
Tel: 1 800 319 9151/1 978 988 3833        Fax: 1 978 988 0233
http://www.nelsonbach.com
Remedies, books, videos and courses.

**Pegasus Products, P.O. Box 228, Boulder, CO, USA 80306**
Tel: 1 800 527 6104.

**Perelandra Flower Essences, Perelandra Center for Nature Research, P.O. Box 3603 Warrenton, VA, USA 22186**
Tel: 1 703 937 2153

# REFERENCES

Andrysko, R. 1989. *Columbus Monthly*. May.

Arehart-Treichel, J. 1982. Pets: The health benefits. *Science News*, 121, 220–4.

Arkow, P. 1984. *Dynamic Relationships in Practice: Animals in the Helping Professions*. Alameda, CA: The Latham Foundation.

Association of Pet Behaviour Counsellors *see* Holmes, J. 1995.

Bach, E. 1931. *Heal Thyself: An Explanation of the Real Cause and Cure of Disease*. London: The C.W. Daniel Co., Ltd.

Bach, E. 1933. *The Twelve Healers*. London: The C.W. Daniel Co., Ltd.

Bach, E. 1933. *The Twelve Healers and the Four Helpers*. London: The C.W. Daniel Co., Ltd.

Bach, E. 1934. *The Twelve Healers and the Seven Helpers*. London: The C.W. Daniel Co., Ltd.

Bach, E. 1936. *The Twelve Healers and Other Remedies*. London: The C.W. Daniel Co., Ltd.

Barnard, J.& Barnard, M. 1996. Flower Essences – preparation of healing herbs. In *The Green Handbook*, Spring Issue, Vol. 3, No. 2, April–June, pp.18–19.

Baun, M.M., Baun, D.N., Thoma, L., Langston, N., Bergstrom, N. 1983. Effects of bonding vs. non-bonding on the physiological effects of petting. *Proceedings of the Conferences on the Human-Animal Bond*. University of Minnesota, June 13–14 1983 and University of California June 17–18, 1983.

Borchelt, P.L. & Voith, V.L. 1982. Diagnosis and treatment of aggression problems in cats. *Veterinary Clinics of North America: Small Animal Practice*. Vol. 12, No. 4, Nov. pp.673–681.

Borchelt, P.L. & Voith, V.L. 1982. Diagnosis and treatment of elimination behavioral problems in cats. In *Veterinary Clinics of North America: Small Animal Practice*. Vol. 12, No. 4, Nov. pp.673–681

Bradshaw, J. 1995. Dominance: What it means to a dog, client and counsellor. Paper presented at the Fourth Annual Symposium of the Association of Pet Behaviour Counsellors, Birmingham. 4th Feb.

Brennan, M.L. with Eckroate, N. 1994. *The Natural Dog: A Complete Guide For Caring Owners*. USA: Plume.

Case, P. 1989. *Natural Remedies Have Growing Appeal For Today's Pet Store Consumer*. Copyright: Penny Case.

Case, P. 1994. Flower Power: The traditional remedies of Dr. Edward Bach. In *Natural Pet*, Nov./Dec. Florida: Pet Publications Inc.

Chancellor, P.M. 1971. *Illustrated Handbook of the Bach Flower Remedies*. Saffron Walden, Essex: C.W. Daniels & Co.

Coren, S. 1994. *The Intelligence of Dogs: Canine Consciousness and Capabilities*. UK: Headline Book Publishing.

Corson, S.A. & O'Leary Corson, E. 1979. Pet animals as nonverbal communication mediators in psychotherapy in institutional settings. In *Ethology and Nonverbal Communication in Mental Health: An Interdisciplinary Biopsychosocial Exploration*. pp.83–110. Oxford: Pergamon.

Corson, S.A., O'Leary Corson, E., Detass, D., Gunsett, R., Gwynne, P.H., Arnold, L.E. & Corson, C.N. 1976. *The Socializing Role of Pet Animals in Nursing Homes: An experiment in non-verbal communication therapy*. UK: Oxford University Press.

Corson, S.A., O'Leary Corson, E., Gwynne, P. & Arnold, L. 1975. Pet-facilitated psychotherapy in a hospital setting. In J.H. Masserman (Ed.) *Current Psychiatric Therapies*. Vol. 15.

Corson, S.A., O'Leary Corson, E., Gwynne, P. & Arnold, L. 1977. Pet dogs as non-verbal communication links in hospital psychiatry. *Comprehensive Psychiatry*. Vol. 18, pp.61–72.

Darwin, C. 1871. *The Descent of Man*. London: Murray.

Darwin, C. 1889. *The Expression of the Emotions in Man and Animals*. 2nd ed. London: Murray.

Durrell, G. 1991. *The Ark's Anniversary*. New York: Arcade Pub.

Fisher, G.T. & Volhard, W. 1985. Puppy personality profile. *American Kennel Gazette*. March.

Fogle, B. 1986. *The Dog's Mind*. London: Pelham.

Fox, M.W. 1985. *Behavior of Wolves, Dogs and Related Canids*. London: Cape.

Frazier, A. with Eckroate, N. 1990. *The New Natural Cat*. Harmondsworth, UK: Penguin.

Friedmann, E., Katcher, A.H., Lynch, J.J. & Thomas, S.A. 1982. Animal companions and one-year survival of patients after discharge from a coronary care unit. *California Veterinarian*. Vol. 8, pp.45–50.

Friedmann, E., Katcher, A.H., Thomas, S.A., Lynch, J.J. & Messent, P.R. 1983 Social interaction and blood pressure: influence of animal companions. *Journal of Nervous and Mental Disease*. Vol. 171, (8) pp.461–465.

Graham, H. 1999. *Complementary Therapies in Context: The Psychology of Healing*. London: Jessica Kingsley.

Graham, H. 1993. Rearing the singular puppy. *Saluki International*. Issue 2, pp.42–3. Cambridge: Ken Allan Publications.

Grossberg, J.M. & Alf, E.F. 1984. *Interaction with pet dogs: Effect on human blood pressure*. Presented at the 92nd Annual Convention of the American Medical Association, Toronto, Canada.

Gurudas. 1983. *Flower Essences and Vibrational Healing*. San Rafael, CA: Cassandra Press.

Harvey, R. 1994. *Psychodermatoses – a veterinary dermatologist's perspective*. Paper given at the annual symposium of the UK Registry of Canine Behaviorists, Oct. 9th. Coventry, UK.

Holden, C. 1981. Human-animal relationship under scrutiny. *Science*. Vol. 214, pp.418–20.

*Holistic Animal News*. Winter 1986. Seattle, WA.

Holmes, J. 1995. Difficult children and difficult dogs (including a report on the fourth annual symposium of the Association of Pet Behaviour Counsellors). *Dog World*. 24th February, p.5.

Jenkins, J. 1984. Physiological Effects of Petting A Companion Animal. Unpublished Masters thesis, San Francisco State University, San Francisco, CA. cited by Pelletier, K.R. & Herzing, D.R. in Psychoneuroimmunology: toward a mind-body model. pp.344–94 in Sheikh, A.S. & Sheikh, K. (eds) *Eastern and Western Approaches to Healing: Ancient Wisdom and Modern Knowledge*. 1989. New York: J. Wiley and Sons.

Jupp, H. 1990. Using the Bach Flower Remedies with dogs. *Dog World*. August 3, p.6.

Kaminski, P. & Katz, R. 1992. *Flower Essence Repertory*. Nevada City, CA: Flower Essence Society.

Kaminski, P. & Katz, R. 1994. *Flower Essence Repertory*. Revised edition. Nevada City, CA: Flower Essence Society.

Kaslof, L.J. 1991. cited in *The Bach Remedies Newsletter*. N.Y: Ellon Bach, USA. Vol. 5, Spring. p.4.

Katcher, A. 1981. Interactions between people and their pets. In Fogle, B.(Ed) *Interrelations Between People and Pets*. Springfield IL: Thomas.

Leigh, M. 1997. Flower Essences. Featherstone, C. & Forsyth, L. (eds). *In Medical Marriage:*

*The New Partnership Between Orthodox and Complementary Medicine.* Findhorn: Findhorn Press.

Mansfield, P. 1995. *Flower Remedies.* UK: Optima.

McCulloch, M.I. 1982. Animal facilitated therapy: an overview. *California Veterinarian.* Vol. 8, pp.13–24.

Morrison, H. 1995. Nature's Prozac. *Natural Health.* May/June. pp.80–128

Mugford, R.A. & McComisky, J.G. 1975. Some recent work on the psychotherapeutic value of caged birds with old people. In Anderson, R.S. (ed) *Pet Animals and Society.* London: Bailliere Tindall.

Muschel, I.J. 1984. Pet therapy with terminal cancer patients. *Journal of Contemporary Social Work.* 451–458.

Pelletier, K.S. & Herzing, D.L. 1989. Psychoneuroimmunology: Towards a mind-body model. In *Eastern and Western Aprpoaches to Healing: Ancient Wisdom and Modern Knowledge.* (eds. A.A. Sheikh & K.S. Sheikh). New York: Wiley.

Pfaffenberger, C.J. 1963. *The New Knowledge of Dog Behavior.* New York: Howell.

Pitcairn, R. 1983. In Kaminski, P. Flower Essences and Animals: An Interview with Richard Pitcairn, DVM, Ph.D. *The Flower Essence Journal.* Issue 4, pp.35–48.

Pitcairn, R.H.& Pitcairn, S.H. 1989. *Natural Health For Dogs and Cats.* London: Prion Books Ltd.

Richardson-Boedler, C. 1994. The catalytic effect of Bach Remedies in Homoeopathic Treatment. *The Homoeopath.* Vol. 54, pp.246–250.

Scarlett, C. 1987. Helping pets help the aged. *Pedigree Digest.* Vol. 14, No.1, pp.5, 11.

Smith, B. 1982. Project Inreach: A program to explore the ability of Atlantic bottlenose dolphins to elicit communication responses from autistic children. In Katcher, A. & Beck, A. (eds) *New Perspectives on Our Life With Companion Animals.* Philadelphia: University of Philadelphia Press.

Stein, D. 1993. *Natural Healing For Dogs and Cats.* Freedom CA: The Crossing Press.

Tuxworth, J. 1981. Is their "Bach" worse than their bite? *Nature and Health.* Vol. 2, No. 4 Spring.

Vlamis, G. 1988. *Flowers To The Rescue: The Healing Vision of Dr. Edward Bach.* Rochester, VT: Healing Arts Press. (First published 1986, Thorsons USA.)

Vlamis, G. 1990. *Bach Flower Remedies To The Rescue.* Rochester, VT. Healing Arts Press.

Vlamis, G. 1994. *Rescue Remedy: The Healing Power of Bach Rescue Remedy.* London: Thorsons.

Voith, V.L. & Borchelt, P.L. 1982. Introduction to Animal Behavior Therapy. Symposium of Animal Behavior. The Veterinary Clinics of North America: *Small Animal Practice.* Vol. 12, No. 4, pp.565–570, Philadelphia: W.B. Saunders Co.

Voith, V.L. 1982. Owner pet attachment despite behavior problems. In Kay, *Pet Loss and Human Bereavement,* p.140.

Weeks, N. 1939. How to cure your pets – The Twelve Healers. In *Health From Herbs Magazine,* March, pp.202, 208.

Weeks, N. 1942. The Twelve Healers and Other Remedies. *New Life: A Quarterly Magazine of Health and Healing* (issued as a Supplement to *The Animal's Companion*). Dec. 1941–1942.

White, I. 1993. *Australian Bush Flower Essences.* Findhorn: Findhorn Press.

Whyte, A.M. 1987. Pets in prisons. *Pedigree Digest.* Vol. 13, No. 4, pp.10–11.

Whyte, P. 1989. Modifying companion-animal dog behavior through touch and communication. In *Companion: Official Journal of the Human/Animal Contact Study Group.* Vol. 6, No. 3, Spring, p.11.

Wright, Small M. 1988. *Flower Essences.* Warrenton, VA: Perelandra, Ltd.

DEEP BOOKS LTD
UNIT 3 GOOSE GREEN TRADING ESTATE
47 EAST DULWICH ROAD
LONDON
SE22 9BN
UK

Thank you for buying this book. If you would like to receive any further information about our product list, please return this card after filling in your areas of interest.

Title of this book...............................................................

If purchased : Retailer's name......................Town.....................

☐ Health and Nutrition      ☐ Philosophy & Spirituality

☐ Indigenous Cultures      ☐ Psychology & Psychotherapy

☐ Occult & Divination      ☐ Women's Interest

☐ Personal Growth      ☐ Other

Name.........................................................................

Address.....................................................................

...................................................................................

# READING LIST

Alaskan Flower Essence Project. 1989. *Flower Essence Studies.* Fairbanks: The Alaskan Flower Essence Project.

Bach, E. & Wheeler, F.J. 1979. *The Bach Flower Remedies.* New Canaan, CT: Keats Publishing Inc.

Bach, E. 1976. *The Twelve Healers and Other Remedies.* Saffron Walden, Essex: C.W. Daniel & Co. Originally published privately in 1933 as *The Twelve Healers.* Revised 1934, revised and enlarged 1936.

Balinski, A. A. 1998. Use of Western Australian flower essences in the management of pain and stress in the hospital setting. *Complementary Therapies in Nursing and Midwifery* Vol. 4, August 1988, pp.111–117.

Barnao, Vasudeva 1988. *Healing With Australian Flowers.* Perth, W. Australia: Living Essences.

Barnard, J. 1979. *The Guide to the Bach Flower Remedies.* Saffron Walden, Essex: C.W. Daniel and Co.

Barnard, J. & Barnard, M. 1988. *The Healing Herbs of Edward Bach: An Illustrated Guide to The Flower Remedies.* Hereford: The Bach Educational Programme.

Barnard, J. 1994. *Collected Writings of Edward Bach.* Bath: Ashgrove Press.

Bellhouse, E. 1985. *Measureless Healing.* Somerset, England: The Elizabeth Bellhouse Foundation.

Brennan, M.L. with N. Eckroate 1994. *The Natural Dog: A Complete Guide For Caring Owners.* USA: Plume.

Case, P. 1994. Flower Power: The traditional remedies of Edward Bach. *Natural Pet.* pp.10–11 November-December.

Chancellor, P.M. 1971. *Illustrated Handbook of the Bach Flower Remedies.* Saffron Walden, Essex: C.W. Daniel and Co.

Cummings, S. 1978. History and development of the bowel nosodes. *J. Homeopathic Practice.* Summer Vol. 1, No. 2, pp.78–89.

Evans, J. 1974. *Introduction to the Benefits of the Bach Flower Remedies.* Saffron Walden, Essex: C.W. Daniel & Co.

Griffin, J. 1989. *Returning To Source.* Fort Worth, Texas: Petite Fleur Essence, Inc.

Gurudas 1983. *Flower Essences and Vibrational Healing.* San Rafael, CA: Cassandra Press.

Harvey, C.G. & Cochrane, A. 1995. *Flower Remedies: the healing power of flower essences from around the world.* London: Thorsons.

Howard, J. & Ramsell, J. 1990. *The Original Writings of Edward Bach.* Saffron Walden: Essex: C.W. Daniel & Co.

Jones, T.H. 1995. *Dictionary of the Bach Flower Essences: Positive and Negative Aspects.* Saffron Walden, Essex: C.W.Daniel Co. (first published by the author, Surrey, England, in 1976).

Johnson, S.M. 1993. *Flower Essences of Alaska.* Homer, Alaska: Alaskan Flower Essence Project.

Johnson, S.M. 1996. *The Essence of Healing: a guide to the Alaskan flower, gem and environmental essences.* Homer, Alaska: Flower Essence Project.

Jupp, H. 1990. Using the Bach Flower Remedies with Dogs. *Dog World.* 3rd August, p.6. Ashford, Kent.

Kaminski, P. 1983. Flower Essences and Animals: An interview with Richard Pitcairn DVM, PhD. *The Flower Essence Journal.* Issue 4, pp.35–42.

Katz, R. & Kaminski, P. 1987. *Healing Today's Child: the Magic of Flower Essences.* Nevada City, CA: The Flower Essence Society (monograph).

Kaminski, P. and Katz, R. 1992. *The Flower Essence Repertory.*Nevada City, CA: The Flower Essence Society.

Kaminski, P. & Katz, R. 1994. *The Flower Essence Repertory.* Revised edition. Nevada City, CA: The Flower Essence Society.

Katz R. & Kaminski, P. 1996. *Flower Essences: Nature's Healing Language.* Nevada City, CA: Flower Essence Services.

Kaslof, L. J. *Traditional Flower Remedies of Edward Bach: A Self-Help Guide.* New Canaan, CT: Keats Publishing.

Kemp, C. 1988. *Flower Essences: Bridges to the Soul.* Tucson, AZ: Desert Alchemy (monograph).

Krishnamurti, V. 1988. *Beginner's Guide to the Bach Flower Remedies.* New Delhi, India: B. Jain Publishers Ltd.

Lindenberg, A. 1988. *Bach-Bluten Therapie Fur Hanstiere: Tierkrankheiten sanft und naturalich heilen.* Tascenbuch ECON. Verlag GmbH, Dusseldorf.

Lopes, T. 1995. In praise of flowers; a talk with holistic therapist Morganna Davies. *Tiger Tribe,* Jan/Feb. pp.32–3.

MacWhinnie, L. 1997. Bach Flower Remedies for Animals. *Homoeopathy International.*V.II Part 2 (Autumn) pp.12–14.

Maly, I. 1991. *Bluten Und Chance Und Hilfe.* Salzburg.

Rotella, A. 1990. *The Essence of Flowers: New Age Wisdom.* Mountain Lakes, NJ: Jade Mountain Press.

Scheffer, M. 1986. *Bach Flower Therapy: Theory and Practice.* London: Thorsons.

Simonds, M.A. 1989. *Essences For Animal Care.* Nevada City,CA: Flower Essence Society (pamphlet).

Starck, M. 1989. *Earth Mother Astrology.* St. Paul, MN: Llewellyn Publications, Inc.

Titchiner, R., Monk, S., Potter, R. & Staines, P. 1997. *New Vibrational Flower Essences of Britain and Ireland.* Suffolk: Waterlily Books.

Vlamis, G. 1988. *Flowers to the Rescue: the healing vision of Dr. Edward Bach.* Rochester, VT: Healing Arts Press.

Vlamis, G. 1990. *Bach Flower Remedies to the Rescue.* Rochester, VT: Healing Arts Press.

Vlamis, G. 1994. *Rescue Remedy: the Healing Power of Bach Rescue Remedy.* London: Thorsons.

Weeks, NB. & Bullen, V. 1964. *The Bach Flower Remedies,Illustrations and Preparation.* Saffron Walden, Essex: C.W. Daniel and Co.

Weeks, N. 1940. *The Medical Discoveries of Edward Bach. Physician: What the Flowers do for the Human Body.* London: The C. W. Daniel Co., Ltd. (or subsequent reprints).

Wheeler, F.J. 1996. *The Bach Remedies Repertory.* Saffron Walden, Essex: C.W. Daniel & Co. (First published 1952).

White, I. 1993. *Australian Bush Flower Essences.* Findhorn, Scotland: Findhorn Press.

Wildwood, C. 1994. *Flower Remedies For Women.* London: Thorsons.

Wood, M. 1987. *Seven Herbs: plants as teachers.* Berkeley, CA: North Atlantic Books.

Wright, M.S. 1988. *Flower Essences.* Warrenton, VA: Perelandra, Ltd.

# INDEX

abscesses 48
absentmindedness 46, 94
abuse *see also* cruelty 43, 60, 86
accident(s) 40, 88, 93
    proneness 44, 89
acne 48
adaptability 57
    lack of 69, 96
adjustment 56, 57, 95
adjuvant therapy 28
adrenal disorders 48
affection 23, 26
Afghan Hounds 49, 82
aged animals 47
    *see* geriatric animals
aggression 8, 39, 62, 71, 77, 78, 96
agony 33
agoraphobia 68
Agrimony 33–5, 94, 97
Akita 57
Alaskan Flower Essences 17
alcohol 91
alertness 47, 94
allergies 38, 39, 48, 49
    acute 55, 74, 81, 83
    stress 50
allopathic medicine 28
aloofness 82, 96
anal gland infection 49
Anatolian Sheepdog 65
Andrysko, Robert 26
anemia 65
anesthesia 81, 88
anesthetic crisis 88
anger 23, 24
anguish 74
annoyance 38
anorexia 72
antibiotics 48
anxiety 14, 26, 34, 35, 37, 68, 84
    excessive 67
    separation 46 54
apathy 53, 85, 96
apologetic behavior 95
appetite 52
    ravenous 72
application 106
applied kinesiology 18
apprehension 35, 94
approval seeking 94
aquatic animals 107
Arabian horses 82, 99
arthritic disorders 38, 60, 70

arthritis 60
Aspen 7, 35–38, 44, 68, 69, 84, 94, 100
aspirin 11
assertiveness 94
    lack of 40, 94
Association of Pet Behaviour Counsellors
    (APBC) 54, 78
asthma 55
astonishment 23
atmospheres 63
attention 23, 47, 59
attention seeking 45, 54, 55, 94
Australian Bush Flower Essences 17
avoidance behaviors 35

Bach Centre, The 18, 19
Bach, Edward 14–16, 17
Bach Flower Remedies 15, 16, 18, 19, 104
back: roaching 33
bad habits 44
Bailey Flower Essences 18
balance 12
    loss of 72, 96
barking 45, 54
Barnard, Julian 19
Barnard, Martine 19
barometric pressure 37
Beech 38, 56, 71, 79, 94
bees 89
behavior inventory 100, 101
behavior problem(s) 8, 27, 42, 54, 77, 80
    characteristics 27
    modification 8
    therapy 8
Bell magpie 72
bitches 54, 55, 57, 62, 73, 85
bites 89, 93
    insect 48, 49
    mites 49, 93
biting
    doors etc 54
    fear 62
    flank 84
    fly 84
    in dogs 45
    owners 55
    tail 84
birds 33, 38, 40, 42, 43, 46, 47, 53, 54, 59
    62, 64, 66, 69, 70, 74, 81, 83, 90, 92, 93
    banding 90
    eggbound 90
    mynah 54
    wild 34

birth 66
contractions 50
difficulties 44, 73, 93
multiple 50
trauma 74
bladder stones 90, 92
bladder weakness 36
bleeding 92
blindness 81
bloat 75
blood pressure 26
blowing 61
Blue Flag essence 17
body
cold 47, 85
heat 33
language 27
postures 77
boiling method, the 15, 16
bone(s)
broken 33
growth 50
splinters 48
boredom 47, 84
Boston Terriers 34
bowels 36, 59
Bradshaw, John, Dr. 78
bravery 68
breathing 35, 88, 92
pattern 33
breed type 99
bruises 90
bruising 91
bucking 43
Bull Terriers 84
Bullen, Victor 16
bullying 40, 77
bumps 93
burn-out see exhaustion
burns 89, 92, 93
butterflies 90

caesarean section 88
California Flower Essences 16, 18
calm 96
Calming Essence 87, 93
Calming Essence Cream 93
calmness 42, 67, 68, 73, 88, 95
calves 75
cancer(s) 35, 53, 57, 60, 63, 64, 66
captivity 60, 75
cardiac arrest 36, 88
cat(s) 33, 36, 38, 44, 46, 47, 51, 52
54, 56, 61, 62, 64, 66, 68, 69, 75, 76
77, 81, 82, 86, 89, 90

cats: copy 41
daydreaming 47
feral 82
oriental 38, 53, 70
Persian 38, 70
owners 26
Siamese 38, 46, 52, 70, 82, 94
semi-feral 82
catteries 37, 52
Cavalier King Charles Spaniel 40
Celestial Remedies 18
central nervous system disease 80
Centaury 40–41
Cerato 15, 27, 41–42, 94
character traits 99
Cherry Plum 42–44, 87, 88
Chestnut Bud 44–45, 52, 53, 59, 76, 84, 94
chewing
furniture 83
paws 83
skin 83
chickens see also poultry 90
Chicory 45–46, 55, 87, 94
Chihuahuas 90
chinchillas 88
chipmunks 90, 105
choking 88, 92
circulatory problems 36
cleanliness 47, 94
cleansing 48, 94
Clematis 46–47, 88, 94
clinging 45
coat: dull 52
coat: matted 48
cockatiels 54
Cocker Spaniels 43, 84
cold 38
body 47, 85
colic 59, 75, 89, 90, 91, 92, 93
collapse 47
Collies 40, 52
Bearded 49
Border 76
competence 50, 94
complementary medicine 28
compliance 94
composure 54, 95
compulsiveness 42, 69, 71, 76, 94
concentration 46
concussion 47
confidence 41, 67, 94, 95
lack of 94
loss of 51, 60, 95
confinement 53
see captivity

confusion                                    80
congestive heart failure                     52
constitutional
    features                           25, 82
    remedies                       34, 43, 99
    type                              35, 100
constipation                         48, 72, 77
contriteness                             67, 95
control                                  42, 94
    loss of                             88, 94
contusions                                   91
convalescence                    40, 41, 65, 83
cooperation                                  58
coping                                       96
    difficulties                             95
coprophagia                                  48
Coren, Stanley Prof.                     21, 24
coma                                         47
courage                              68, 94, 95
coursing                                 51, 64
cowering                                 35, 36
cows                                    68, 106
coyote                                       82
Crab Apple        7, 35, 47–50, 77, 83
                                     84, 86, 94
cramp                                        59
craziness                                    42
crime                                       101
cruciate ligaments (ruptured)            65, 76
cruelty                                  73, 75
        see abuse
Crystal Herbs Emergency Essence      87, 93
Crystal Herbs Emergency Essence Cream  93
curiosity                                    23
currawong                                    72
cystitis                                     36

Dachshunds                                   39
dandruff                                     48
Darwin, Charles                      21, 23, 24
deafness                                     81
decomposition                                49
defecation                           33, 34, 50
    involuntary                              47
defiance                                     55
degenerative myopathy                    49, 64
dental treatment                         69, 88
depression                           62, 63, 95
dermatitis                                   48
despair                                      95
despondency                              52, 53
destructive behavior         43, 45, 54, 86
devotion                                     23
diabetes                                     48
diabetic dogs            73, 74, 89, 90, 92

diarrhea                 36, 46, 47, 59, 72
dietary change                           48, 81
digestive upset(s)                       33, 36
dignity                                  47, 94
dilated pupils                               33
dingo                                        82
discouragement                           52, 95
disease
    degenerative                            60
    musculoskeletal                         60
disgust                                      18
disinterest                                  46
dislike                                      95
distemper                                    65
distress             33, 43, 49, 80, 88
    concealed                                94
    intense                                  96
Dobermans                                46, 84
dogs        34, 35, 39, 42, 44, 46, 47, 49, 51
            52, 53, 54, 57, 59, 64, 66, 68, 70
                        73, 76, 77, 83, 90
    army                                 51, 58
    bomb squad                               52
    competition                          61, 66
    coursing                                 51
    diabetic            73, 74, 89, 90, 92
    drug search                              51
    dual purpose                             85
    guard                                85, 99
    guide                            24, 42, 52
    hearing                              25, 51
    herding                              59, 65
    hunting                              40, 42
    kennel                                   55
    mountain rescue                          51
    obedience                                24
    police                   25, 42, 51, 58
    pushy                                    59
    racing                                   51
    rescue                               66, 85
    search and rescue                    66, 85
    show                                  62, 85
    sled                                 52, 59
    stud                                     42
    sporting                                 65
    travellers'                              65
    working                      24, 51, 58, 65
    working trial                            42
dominance            38, 69, 71, 77, 96
dosage                               105–108
dove                                         90
dowsing                                      18
drinking: excessive                          58
drowsiness                                   47
dung-eating                                  48

| | |
|---|---|
| Durrell, Gerald | 21 |
| dyes | 43 |
| | |
| ears | |
|     disorders | 92 |
|     down | 35, 62 |
|     infection | 43 |
|     mites | 43 |
|     pressed to head | 40 |
|     problems | 75 |
| eating problems | 52, 70 |
|     see also anorexia, appetite | |
|     and dung-eating | |
| eczema | 48, 59 |
| electromagnetic fields | 102 |
| elimination problems | 81, 86 |
|     see also constipation | |
| Ellon Traditional Flower Remedies | 18 |
| Ellon, USA | 18, 87 |
| Elm | 7, 50–51, 95 |
| emergency remedies | 87–93 |
|     treatment | 68 |
| emotion(s) | 14, 21, 22, 24, 102 |
| endurance | 41, 51, 53, 64, 95, 96 |
| energy | 12, 76 |
|     field(s) | 13, 14 |
|     imbalance(s) | 13 |
|     levels | 15 |
|     lack | 85 |
|     low | 53 |
| environment | 34, 37, 40, 56, 63 |
| epilepsy | 43 |
| epileptic fits | 47 |
| euthanasia | 42, 43, 51, 56, 73, 78, 81 |
| eventers | 40, 42, 52 |
| exhaustion | 47, 50, 65, 89, 91, 95 |
| exposure | 91, 93 |
| expression | |
|     hang-dog | 62 |
|     fearful | 35 |
|     pained | 33 |
|     shifty | 34 |
|     spacy | 47 |
|     vacant | 47 |
| eye(s) | |
|     downcast | 62 |
|     loss | 81 |
|     running | 49 |
| | |
| fainting | 47 |
| faintness | 48 |
| false pregnancy | 73, 85 |
| fasting | 48 |
| fatigue | 65, 95 |
| fear(s) | 23, 24, 37, 43, 67 |
| fear: being clipped | 62 |
|     being shod | 62 |
|     biting | 62 |
|     dark | 62 |
|     dogs | 62 |
|     extreme | 68, 94 |
|     failure | 60 |
|     fireworks | 62 |
|     irrational | 37 |
|     known things | 61, 94, 95 |
|     lightening | 93 |
|     shadows | 62 |
|     starting pistols | 62 |
|     starting traps | 62 |
|     thunderstorms | 62, 100 |
|     trains | 62 |
|     travel | 62 |
|     unknown things | 35–37, 94 |
| feathers | 43 |
|     removing | 62 |
| feeding mistakes | 40 |
| feet | 53, 90 |
|     thorns in | 33 |
| feline leukemia | 52, 66 |
| fever | 11, 55 |
| finches | 90 |
| first aid | 44 |
| fish | 90, 93, 107 |
| fits see epilepsy, epileptic fits | |
| flea(s) | 48, 84 |
|     allergy | 49 |
| fledglings | 90 |
| flexibility | 38, 39, 69, 94 |
| flower(s) | 11, 12, 13, 14 |
| flower essence summary chart | 94 |
| Flower Essence Society (FES) | 16, 17 |
| fluctuating features | 72, 96 |
| foals | 91 |
| focus | 46 |
|     lack of | 47 |
| Fogle, Bruce | 27, 54 |
| food | |
|     additives | 43 |
|     no interest in | 52, 85 |
| forebrain lesions | 80 |
| foreign bodies | 48, 50, 82, 83 |
| Fox, Michael | 27 |
| fractures | 65, 76, 92 |
| frenzy | 43, 69 |
| fright | 43 |
| frothing at mouth | 61 |
| fungal infections | 44 |
| fur ball | 48 |
| | |
| gastrointestinal problems | 36, 59 |

Gentian 52–53, 87, 95
gentleness 69
gerbils 106
geriatric animals 51, 66, 81
    *see* aged animals
German Shepherds 46
ghost(s) 37
    giving up 70
giddiness 68
glands 49
Global Health Alternatives 18, 19
    *see* Traditional Flower Remedies From
Ellon and Ellon Traditional Flower Remedies
gloom 62
gloominess 95
goats 49, 106
Golden Retrievers 34
Gorse 52, 53, 95
granulomas 48
Great Danes 106
Greyfriars Bobby 57
greyhounds 59, 62, 85
grief 23, 24, 73
    obsessive 48
groaning 54
grooming 89, 90
    *see* overgrooming
growling 55
guide dogs 24, 27
guide dog training program 25
guilt 67
guinea pigs 106
gun-shyness 51
gums 91
Gurudas 17

hackles 39
Hahnemann, Samuel 12, 14, 15
hair
    chewing 46
    loss 48, 56
    pulling out 46, 48
    raising 39
hamsters 35, 51, 65, 106
Harvey, Richard 84
healing 11, 12
heart
    attack 91
    disorders 61, 64
    failure 92
    rate 26, 46, 94
heat 38
    constant (in cats) 64
    commencing 80
    stroke 89, 92

Heather 54–55, 95
hedgehog(s) 49, 66
Healing Herbs English Flower Essences
16, 19
Healing Herbs Five Flower Remedy 87, 93
herd animals 42
hesitancy 60, 95
hibernation 65, 66
hindquarters 33
hip dysplasia 49, 60
Holly 39, 55–56, 95, 106
homeopathic remedies 17, 27, 29, 107, 108
homeopathy 12, 15, 108
    and flower essences 13
homesickness 56, 95
Honeysuckle 56–57, 81, 86, 87, 95
hopelessness 52, 53, 95
hormone(s) 14
    imbalance 63, 72
Hornbeam 57–58, 66, 95
horses 35, 36, 39, 40, 42, 45, 46, 47, 49
    51, 52, 53, 54, 55, 60, 61, 62, 64
    66, 68, 69, 70, 74, 75, 76, 81, 82
    85, 86, 87, 90
    Arabian 82, 99
    arthritic 60
    biting 43
    bucking 43
    dressage 39, 64
    eventing (*see* eventers) 42
    hunting 40, 42
    kicking 55
    police 51
    showjumping 42
    team 60
    tense 39
Howard, Judy 16
human-animal bond 26–28
humidity 38
Huskies 82
hyperactivity 76, 96
hyperthyroidism 86
hypochondriachal behavior 70
hysterectomy 52
hysteria 88, 95

imbalance 72, 96
    chemical 63
    hormones 63, 72
imitative behavior 41
impatience 14, 58, 88, 95
Impatiens 58–60, 84, 88, 95
impulsiveness 76, 96
inactivity
    enforced 57

inadequacy 50, 94
inattentiveness 95
incontinence 43, 47
incubation 83
indifference 96
indigestion 59
individuality 40
infection(s) 40, 47, 48
    severe 55, 94
infirmity 65
inflammation 93
inflexibility 38, 69, 70
initiative 41
    lack of 41
injury 88, 89
insects 91
    bites 48, 49
insecticides 48
intolerance 38, 58, 94
intuitive diagnosis 18
Irish Setter 63
Irish Wolfhounds 35, 90, 99, 106
irritable bowel syndrome 36, 59
irritability 58, 60, 88, 95
itchiness 49
itching 59, 92

jealousy 23
Johnson, Steve 17
juvenile behavior 41

Kaminski, Patricia 14, 16
Kaslof, Leslie 18, 104
Kaslof, Ralph 18
Katz, Richard 14, 16
kennel(s) 37, 52, 85, 87
    dogs 55
keynote(s) 17, 94–96, 100
kicks 55
kidney disease 47
kidney stones 90

labor 91
Labradors 40, 59, 84
lambs 25, 26, 91
laminitis 53
Larch 37, 40, 41, 51, 52, 60–61, 95
larynx 88
leadership 96
learning difficulties 69, 94
legs 65
leg splinting 90
lethargy 53
leukemia 53
Lhasa Apsos 49

licking: constant 40, 48, 49, 83
licking: excessive 43, 46
lick sores 48
life force 85, 91
limb loss 81
listlessness 47, 52, 58
litters: large 50
liver disease 41, 48
London Homoeopathic Hospital 15
loneliness 54, 95
look see expression
lotions 107
lotus 11, 12
    flower 12
love 23, 24
Lovell, David 18

macaws 54
malice 95
maliciousness 55, 86, 96
mange 48, 49
    see sarcoptic mange
Mansfield, Peter 17, 19
mares 46, 91
marine animals 107
marital problems 34
mating 91
    difficulties 41
memory dysfunction 47
mental attitude 17, 77, 95
miaowing 54
miasm 12
    see vibrational pattern
mice 65, 106
Mimulus 36, 37, 61–62, 69, 78, 84, 95, 100
mind 21, 22, 23
mood 99, 100
    remedies 99
mother tincture 16
motion sickness 72
Murray, Nickie 16
muscle
    tension 33, 35, 39, 59, 60, 88
    testing 18
    torn 65
Mustard 11, 62–63, 95
mules 60
mynah birds 54

needs 101–102
needles (in limbs) 33
neglect 75
nerve function 49
nervous conditions 76

nervousness 35, 61, 89–92, 95
neutering 80
noisiness 95
nonverbal communication 27
nosebleed 92
nose running 49
nosode(s) 15
nostrils flaring 61, 91
numbness 74

Oak 35, 41, 51, 52, 64–65, 71, 95
obedience
  champions 85
  dogs 24
  instructors 24
obesity 27
obsessional behaviors 64, 83
obstructions 48
oil slick 65
  poisoning 66
Old English Sheepdogs 49
Olive 15, 41, 58, 64, 65–66, 71, 75, 95
orientals 38
orthopedic correction 52
  injury 52
overattachment 54
overconcern 95
overenthusiasm 76, 96
overgrooming 36, 48, 49
overprotectiveness 46, 67, 77–78, 95
owners
  abusive 41
  anxious 68
  disappointed 53
  dominant 80
  hypochondriachal 68
  impatient 60
  intolerant 39
  macho 80
  nervous 38
  strong-willed 41
  tyrannical 80
  uncertain 42

pacing 61
pack animals 55
Paige, Doreen 18
pain 11, 23, 33, 34
pain: chronic 80, 93
  intense 96
  severe 55, 59, 60, 88
pancreatitis 92
panic 36, 43, 69, 88
panting 35, 61, 94
paralysis 39, 89, 92

parasites 40, 48, 49
parrots 42, 54, 59, 62, 64
parvovirus 58
patience 58, 95
paws
  chewing 83
  sweating 83
  thorns in 33
pecking 38
peck order 40
Pegasus Products 17
Pekinese 59
Perelandra Flower Essences 18
perseverance 52, 53, 74, 95
Persian cats 38
persistence 95
personality 24
  characteristics 25
pet sitters 37
Pfaffenberger, Clarence 24, 25
phantom pregnancy 73, 85
phobias 43, 62
  recurring 94
pigeons 66
Pine 67, 95
pining 56
Pitcairn, Richard 24
poisoning 48, 66, 69, 74, 89, 92, 94
pollution 64, 66
ponies 40
  Exmoor 99
  Connemara 99
  pit 75
  polo 42, 57
  Shetland 99
poodles 49
possessiveness 45, 94
postures 77
poultry 69, 72
prancing 81
pregnancy 80
  see false and phantom
preoccupation 83, 99
protectiveness 45, 46
psychomotor seizures 43, 72
psychoneuroimmunology (PNI) 14
puffing 61
pulse points 91
puppies 55, 57, 61, 68, 79, 81
  solo 55
purring 33
  for attention 54
pustules 49
pyometra 58

Queensland Itch 49

rabbits 88, 91, 106
rabies
    see vaccination
racehorses 43, 51, 58, 62, 85, 90
Radiation Remedy 87
rain 38
Ramsell, John 16
ravens 90
rearing (in horses) 36, 39
reassurance 88
rebalancing 72
recuperation 83
recurrent sickness 44
Red Chestnut 67–68, 95
relapse 52, 53, 56, 72
repetitive behavior 44, 84, 94
repression 69, 96
reproductive problems 42
    see mating
rescued animals 89
Rescue Remedy 44, 46, 50, 72, 87–93
Rescue Remedy Cream 49, 91, 102
relaxation 88
reserve 82, 96
resignation 63, 85, 96
resilience 64, 95
    lack of 95
resistance 40, 50, 60, 94
resonance 12, 15
    sympathetic 27
rest 83
restlessness 61, 84, 96
restraint 61, 96
revitalization 47, 56, 66
rheumatic disorders 83
riders: disabled 51
rigidity 39, 61, 69, 96
roaching (back/loin) 33
Rock Rose 62, 68–69, 71, 87, 88, 95
Rock Water 39, 45, 57, 69–71, 96
rodents 65, 90
Rottweilers 46
routine 58
rushing 61
ruthlessness 38
saddle sores 9
Salukis 64, 78, 82, 99
sarcoptic mange 50
scab 49
scabies 50
scale 48
Scleranthus 72–73, 87

scratching 48
    persistent 83
    walls/furniture 36, 38, 44
seabirds 64, 66
seances 63
sebaceous glands 49
sedatives 88
seizures 47, 65
    psychomotor 72
    anticipation of 37
self-assurance 41
    lack of 41
self-denying behavior 70
self-destructive behavior 43, 46, 75
separation problems 46, 54, 67, 73, 93
senility 47, 83
sensitivity 39
serenity 62, 95
servility 40
setback 95
shaking 35
shame 23
sheep 45, 49, 86, 106
Shih Tzus 49
shock 35, 47, 72, 73–74, 91, 93, 96
shyness (in horses) 36, 61
Siamese cats 38, 46, 52, 70
skin
    chewing 83
    diseases 48, 50, 56, 75
    chronic 83, 84
    eruptive 81
    irritation(s) 33, 49, 59
    tearing 43, 75
Skye Terrier 49
sleeplessness 83, 96
snakebite 89, 92
sneezing 89, 92
snorting 35, 61
sows 73
spaciness 88
spinal disc prolapse 39
spine degeneration 49, 64
spirits see ghosts 37
    low 62, 63
spitefulness 86, 96
splinters 48
spondylitis 49
spontaneity 96
sprains 93
spraying 38, 61, 70, 81
    see urination
sprays 106
Springer Spaniels 76
squirrels 88, 90, 106

stability 95
stallions 91
stamina 64, 65, 71
Star of Bethlehem 35, 73–74, 87, 88
96, 107
starvation 73, 75
St. Bernards 106
steroids 48
stoicism 64
stomach upsets 41
see digestive disorders
storage 105
strangers 93
strays 61
strength 64, 77, 95
stress 34, 35, 40, 50, 52, 69, 84
86, 88, 89, 93
competition 93
reactions 91
stubbornness 39, 70
stud tail 49
submission 37, 67
submissiveness 37, 79, 94
submissive postures 40
sudden collapse 89, 92
suicidal behavior 43
sulkiness 23, 86
sulking 45
Sun Essences 87, 93
sun method, the 15, 18
sunstroke 68
suppleness 69, 96
surgery 47, 48, 65, 74, 87, 88, 93
suspiciousness 55
sweating 35, 61
Sweet Chestnut 74–75
swelling 93
synchronization 12, 14

Tabor, Mary 16
tail
down 35, 36, 49
lashing 83
stud 49
wagging 34, 35, 36
tartar 48
team animals 58
teething 80
temper: bad 55, 94
temper: tantrums 27
temperament 24
good 96
schizophrenic 96
uncertain 72
temperature fluctuations 72

tension 26, 59, 76, 88, 89
see muscles
terminal conditions 53
terriers 76
territorial behavior (territoriality) 69, 77–78
territory 39, 65
terror 23
thorns 33
thunder 93
ticks 48
tightness 69, 96
timidity 61
tiredness 57, 64, 66
toilet control 54
tolerance 55, 94
tongue 89
torsion 89, 90
tortoises 66
touch 38, 47
toxicity 47
Traditional Flower Remedies From Ellon 18
see Global Health Alternatives,
Ellon Traditional Flower Remedies
training 50, 51, 52, 58, 89
difficulties 47, 69
transition 81
transportation 81
tranquilizers 88, 91
trauma 60, 73, 88, 96
travelling 90
travel sickness 70
trembling 35
trust 95
tumors 80
Tuxworth, John 49, 53, 59
type 99
remedies 99
see constitutional

uncertainty 72, 96
uncleanliness 47, 54, 94
unconsciousness 47, 68, 88
uncontrollable behavior 94
unresponsiveness 95
unsteadiness 61
urination 33, 34, 35, 40, 43, 44, 50, 70
inappropriate 86
submissive 37
see spraying
urticaria 55

vaccination 83
vaccines – bacterial 15
vertigo 72
Vervain 49, 76, 96

vibration(s)     13, 14
vibrational
    character     12, 13, 15
    healing     17
    pattern     12
    *see* miasms
viciousness     55
Vine     15, 37, 39, 41, 77–80, 87, 96
vitality     53, 57, 95
vitamin C     66
Vlamis, Gregory     29, 32
Volhard Jack     25
Volhard Wendy     25
vomiting     45, 46, 59

waking     47
Walnut     37, 57, 71, 73, 80–81, 84, 87, 96
Water Violet     50, 66, 82–83, 96, 99
weakness     52, 57, 64, 95
weaning     45, 67
    delay     80
weariness     57
Weeks, Nora     16
weight loss     48, 59
Westlake, Aubrey     87
Wheeler, Dr. F. J.     16
whimpering     36
whining     54

White Chestnut     46, 49, 83–84, 87, 96
White, Ian     17
wild animals     34, 60, 69, 74, 75
Wild Oat     84–85, 87, 96, 107
Wild Rose     52, 63, 85–86, 98
Willow     39, 86, 96
will to live     85, 96
wind     49
wing(s)     53, 72
    wrapping     90
withdrawal     50, 83
wolf     82
womb disease     57
worm infestation     48
worry     14
wound(s)     89
    cleansing     48, 91
    debriding     90
    gunshot     92
Wright, Machaelle Small     18

X-ray     35

yapping     54
Yorkshire Terriers     90

zoos     85

# Also from Findhorn Press

### FINDHORN FLOWER ESSENCES

*Marion Leigh*

Marion explains the theory, preparation and practical applications of the flower essences. The book also includes a thorough, indexed repertoire of illnesses and their indicated treatments.

£9.95/US$16.95 Pbk 128 pages (+ 16 pages in colour)

ISBN 1 899171 96 7

### AMAZONIAN GEM & ORCHID ESSENCES

*Andreas Korte, Antje & Helmut Hofmann*

The vibratory qualities of Amazonian gems and orchids have been extracted for their therapeutic effects. This book describes each of the essences and its applications.

£9.95/US$16.95 Pbk 116 pages

(inc. 40 detachable colour cards)

ISBN 1 899171 91 6

### AUSTRALIAN BUSH FLOWER ESSENCES

*Ian White*

An informative yet personal picture of fifty bush flower essences and detailed information about their preparation and use in all areas of healing. Fully illustrated. The Australian Bush Flower Essences themselves are available in the UK and many other countries.

£11.95/US$19.95 Pbk 210 pages (+16 pages in colour)

ISBN 0 905249 84 4

**FINDHORN** *Press*

Findhorn Press is the publishing business of the Findhorn Community which has grown around the Findhorn Foundation in northern Scotland.

For further information about the Findhorn Foundation and the Findhorn Community, please contact:

## Findhorn Foundation
The Visitors Centre
The Park, Findhorn IV36 3TY, Scotland, UK
tel 01309 690311• fax 01309 691301
email reception@findhorn.org
www.findhorn.org

For a complete Findhorn Press catalogue, please contact:

## Findhorn Press

The Park, Findhorn,
Forres IV36 3TY
Scotland, UK
Tel 01309 690582

Fax 01309 690036

P. O. Box 13939
Tallahassee
Florida 32317-3939, USA
Tel (850) 893 2920
toll-free 1-877-390-4425
Fax (850) 893 3442

e-mail info@findhornpress.com
http://www.findhornpress.com